THE NIMROD

Martyn Chorlton

AMBERLEY

Acknowledgments

Thanks to Stewart Davidson for helping source a large number of the photographs in this book via the late R. L. Ward Collection, and thanks also to Andy King and Chris Hearn.

First published 2020

Amberley Publishing
The Hill, Stroud, Gloucestershire, GL5 4EP
www.amberley-books.com

Copyright © Martyn Chorlton, 2020

The right of Martyn Chorlton to be identified as the
Author of this work has been asserted in accordance with
the Copyright, Designs and Patents Act 1988.

ISBN 978 1 4456 9804 5 (print)
ISBN 978 1 4456 9805 2 (ebook)

British Library Cataloguing in Publication Data.
A catalogue record for this book is available from the
British Library.

Typesetting by Aura Technology and Software
Services, India. Printed in Great Britain.

Contents

Maritime Reconnaissance

The use of aircraft to help protect our shores and sovereign seas began, appropriately, at the beginning, with the foundation of the Royal Naval Air Service (RNAS) in 1912. Coastal and anti-submarine patrols came to the fore during the First World War, these tasks being carried out by normal land-based aircraft, flying boats and airships, the latter enjoying an extensive endurance. There were a number of attacks (107 in 1917 alone) by RNAS, Royal Flying Corps, RFC and later RAF aircraft during the First World War, but the real success was the potential threat posed by the aircraft: when an aircraft was spotted, the enemy submarine had no choice but to dive below periscope depth, where it posed no harm.

Shackleton Replacement

Even though the Shackleton had only been in RAF service for five years, in 1956 the process began to prepare for a replacement. Simultaneously, several NATO countries which had been supplied the US-built Lockheed Neptune, including the RAF as an interim, began the same task. In the meantime, the French were just getting on with designing their own maritime patrol aircraft, in the shape of the Bréguet 1150, better known as the Atlantic. A number of other proposals were submitted to NATO but the Atlantic beat the competition hands down and was bought without hesitation by the French, Germans and, later, the Dutch and the Italians. Equally unsurprising was the rejection by the RAF of the Atlantic, citing a lack of advanced technology and an apparent risk of corrosion; the latter was never suffered right up to the first variant of the aircraft retiring in the 1990s (as the Atlantique 2, the aircraft is still very much in service with the Aéronavale). One idea that failed was submitted by Avro, who approached Bréguet with a proposed modified Atlantic, designated the Avro-Bréguet 2A. The aircraft was to be fitted with an extra pair of Rolls-Royce RB.153-61 jet engines, mounted in under-wing pods. Additional fuel was to be carried in tip tanks, but unfortunately the joint project never got off the drawing board thanks to differences on how the fuselage was constructed. Avro also proposed the Avro 775, a maritime reconnaissance aircraft designed to replace the Shackleton. Power was to be provided by two Rolls-Royce Tyne turboprops and a single rear-mounted Rolls-Royce RB.168 turbofan; once again, the Avro 775 remained nothing more than lines on paper.

A more specific approach was needed and on 18 July 1960 the RAF issued OR (Operational Requirement) 350 for a maritime patrol aircraft which was to be in service by 1968. In 1961, little mention was given to a cautious proposal by Hawker Siddeley for a 'Maritime Comet', an idea that would only resurface again when the number of engines required to operate at low level would come to the fore several years later. OR.350 was followed in June 1963 by OR.357, which basically called for a maritime reconnaissance aircraft with greater performance than the Atlantic, including a transit/cruising speed of 450 kts, a capability of operating at 180 kts over an eight-hour period up to 1,000 miles from home and be able to carry up to 18,620 lb of stores.

The two main British aircraft manufacturing groups at that time, BAC and Hawker Siddeley, presented a number of proposals on the back of OR.357. BAC presented a RB.177-22-powered version of the VC10, a maritime reconnaissance version of the Vickers Vanguard, a similarly converted variant of a Canadair CL-44 and the most ambitious: a swing-wing, Mach 2-capable aircraft powered by reheated versions of the RB.177. Hawker Siddeley's multiple proposals included the Avro 776 with a trio of rear-mounted RB.178 turbofans, the Trident MR.1 and MR.2, the AW.681 MR.1 and MR.2, the Avro 784 powered by four turboprops and, just like BAC's daring proposal, a high-speed swing-wing design. At this stage the Avro 776, which was heavily based upon the HS.121 Trident, was the front runner, purely because it was the only design which could achieve all of OR.357s requirements.

The goalposts were moved again on 4 June 1964 when ASR.381 was issued with the fact that the 1968 deadline was rapidly approaching and the idea of an 'interim' replacement for the Shackleton had to be considered. Once again, ASR.381 was heavily based on the 'interim' either being or being very much like the Atlantic. ASR.381 was a less demanding requirement but it still needed the Shackleton replacement to be able to carry out the following tasks: deal with submarines both on the surface and underwater, be able to carry nuclear and conventional weapons, carry out large-area surveillance, perform air-to-surface attacks, shadow enemy surface ships and finally be equipped for ASR duties. RAF St Mawgan hosted a trial of the four 'already operational' main contenders in 1964. An example of a Vickers Vanguard, Vickers VC10, de Havilland Comet and Hawker Siddeley Trident were each put through their paces on simulated sorties. This involved low-level speed trials, fuel consumption, ride comfort, crew accommodation and many other tests.

The Air Ministry now found itself in a position where only an interim design could be introduced: one which should be capable of carrying out the present Shackleton duties but have enough legs in the design to improve it if need be. All proposed designs were now off the table and only BAC's VC10 and Hawker Siddeley's two Trident proposals, the MR.1 and MR.2, were being seriously looked at. The VC10 quickly fell by the wayside thanks to its size and potential operating costs, leaving just the two Tridents. However, Hawker Siddeley had not forgotten about the idea of a 'Maritime Comet', playing on the fact that

The Avro Shackleton pictured here was the MR.3 variant, in service with No. 206 Squadron. It was this aircraft that was destined to be replaced by the Hawker Siddeley Nimrod. (Crown Copyright via Chris Hearn)

Above: The Dassault-Bréguet Atlantic, a contender as a Shackleton replacement that failed to be selected thanks to only having two, rather than the RAF's required four, engines. (Avions Marcel Dassault-Bréguet Aviation)

Right: The front runner for the RAF's new maritime patrol aircraft was the Avro 776; in the end, the design never left the drawing board.

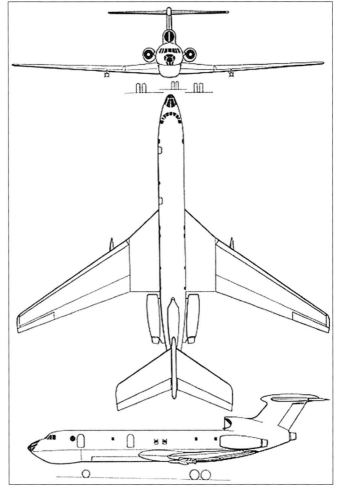

the RAF were not keen on any aircraft with less than four engines operating at low level over the sea.

Designated the HS.801, Hawker Siddeley's design was heavily based on the Comet 4 airliner but instead of Rolls-Royce Avon engines, Speys would be installed instead. All the performance numbers fitted the requirement and the extra power produced by the Spey engine would give the aircraft sufficient range and fuel efficiency to not only equal the Shackleton, but more than surpass it. It was all falling into place for Hawker Siddeley, which still retained all of the original Comet tooling and on top of that, they even had a couple of spare unsold airframes at Hawarden, Chester, which could serve as prototypes, making the 'Maritime Comet' the perfect interim solution. Even though it was designed in the 1940s, the Comet's wing was efficient throughout the flight envelope and from a pilot's point of view the aircraft handled well while from the crew's perspective it was a comfortable aircraft to operate in. The ability to shut down up to three of the Comet's four engines to extend endurance was one of several clinching factors that saw it chosen as the Shackleton replacement. Such was the power of the Spey, it was calculated that the HS.801 would be able to climb to 5,000 ft on a single engine at a weight of approximately 150,000 lb!

In typical British style, that interim would go on to serve for more than four decades.

Cancellations and Orders

1965 was a pretty tough year for Hawker Siddeley; it began with the cancellation of two major potential aircraft, namely the supersonic P.1154 V/STOL fighter and the HS.681 (aka Armstrong Whitworth AW.681) long-range STOL transport aircraft. These cancellations were announced by the Prime Minister, Harold Wilson, in February 1965, but in the same speech he also announced that the 'Maritime Comet' would be ordered for the RAF. The latter news was more bittersweet as an order for the HS.801 alone could not save the old Armstrong Whitworth factory at Baginton, Coventry, plus a large number of redundancies across the Hawker Siddeley group, which totalled a shattering 7,700 workers.

Approval to proceed with the HS.801 was officially given to Hawker Siddeley in the summer of 1965, and even then further work was needed to refine the design, which included new engine intakes from those suited to the Avon to the smaller aperture needed for the Spey. By late 1965, the exact specifications of the HS.801 were ready and on 31 December 1965 a contract to supply two prototype aircraft and thirty-eight production aircraft (to be serialled XV226 to XV263), valued at £95 million, was signed. These aircraft would replace the Shackleton MR.2 fleet only; the MR.3s would continue without replacement, the last of them departing No. 203 Squadron at Luqa, Malta, from December 1971.

Nuts and Bolts of the Nimrod

Hawker Siddeley wasted no time; let's face it – they had no time to waste as once the contract had been signed, the RAF were expecting their new Nimrod to be in service within a mere forty-eight months. The availability of the two unsold Comet 4C airframes (construction Nos 06476 and 06477) provided a huge advantage with regard to progressing the aircraft as quickly as possible to the flight stage. These two prototype aircraft were allocated the RAF serials XV147 (c/n 06476) and XV148 (c/n 06477), the latter destined to be the first aerodynamic prototype, while the former would be the systems prototype. In the meantime, some of the Comet tooling was moved from Hawarden to Chadderton (sub-assemblies), Hatfield (engine intakes and tailplane) and Woodford (final assembly and flight testing), while the actual conversion of the prototype aircraft would be carried out at Hawarden along with construction of the wing centre sections. XV148 was fitted with a new wing section to accommodate four Spey engines, while XV147, which was already three-quarters built as a Comet 4C, retained the original Avon 525B engines. On 23 May 1967, HS.801 XV148 performed its short maiden flight – with John Cunningham and Jimmy Harrison in the cockpit – from Hawarden to Woodford, the aircraft only then being officially referred to as the Nimrod. Prior to this, XV147, once again with Cunningham and Harrison at the controls, departed Hawarden for Woodford on 25 October 1965, a less momentous occasion because the aircraft looked like a standard Comet 4C. XV147 would re-emerge as the second Nimrod MR.1 prototype complete with Spey engines in July 1967.

The fuselage of the Nimrod is 6 ft 6 in. shorter than the original Comet 4C thanks to the removal of a section forward of the main wing. As already mentioned, the wing centre section was completely redesigned to accommodate four RB.168 Spey 250 engines neatly between the two main spars. Both the port and starboard outer Spey engines are fitted with thrust reverser buckets and the engines were treated to help stave off salt-water corrosion. The electrical equipment requires a great deal of power, and to handle this each engine was fitted with a 60kVA constant-speed alternator. Below the fuselage was attached a vast unpressurized section which created a pair of huge weapons bays, totalling 48 ft 6 in. in length. This incredibly aerodynamic lower fuselage section gives the aircraft its distinctive 'double-bubble' shape and can accommodate six lateral rows of attachment points for virtually every airborne store used by the RAF. Alternatively, these points can be used for up to six auxiliary fuel tanks.

An EMI ASV-21D surveillance radar (as installed in the Shackleton) filled the nose of the Nimrod, located outside of the pressurized fuselage and in front of the unpressurized section. To the rear of the latter section are additional fuel tanks which contribute to a total capacity of 10,730 gallons (48,780 lts). The landing gear was beefed up to take the extra weight of the Nimrod, and to compensate for the increased surface area of the fuselage a dorsal fin was fitted to improve lateral and directional control.

The tail also looked different from a standard Comet thanks to a large ESM blister mounted on top and the profile continues to differ with the fitment of a long MAD (Magnetic Anomaly Detector) tailboom. The MAD was multi-functioning and could provide information on hostile radio and radar signals, not to mention their bearing, range and characteristics. The production MR.1 used a Thomson-CSF electronic support measures system to receive and interpret the information from the MAD. The MAD itself was made by the US company Emerson Electronics and consists of a very sensitive magnetometer positioned as far aft from the all-metal fuselage as is physically possible, so it can detect even the slightest perturbation created by a submarine under the surface to the Earth's magnetic field. The bulk of the rear fuselage was used for the storage of sonobouys (including the location of the ejectors), marine markers and various other stores. Another anti-submarine device installed in the early aircraft was an Autolycus diesel exhaust 'sniffer' fitted into the roof of the flight deck. Another useful and powerful tool was a 70 million candle power searchlight which was fitted into the nose of the starboard external fuel tank and was operated by the co-pilot.

The tactical compartment takes up all of the remaining above-floor space from the rear of the cockpit to the galley amidships. The windows are a narrower, 'eyebrow' shape compared to the Comet and the glass panels are deeper. The original mission crew of the MR.1 was made up of a routine navigator, tactical navigator, radio operator, a pair of

One of two Comet 4C airframes that served as prototype Nimrod aircraft. (R. L. Ward Collection)

Hawker Siddeley Nimrod XV148, the first prototype aircraft. (Hawker Siddeley Aviation Ltd via R. L. Ward Collection)

Despite being a long-serving prototype, images of XV147 are sparse. This is the second prototype Nimrod during service with MoD(PE) in late 1982. (R. L. Ward Collection)

Above: Nimrod production begins at Woodford. (Hawker Siddeley Aviation Ltd via R. L. Ward Collection)

Right: A nacelle tank tail fairing for a Nimrod MR.1 under production at Woodford. (Hawker Siddeley Aviation Ltd via R. L. Ward Collection)

No. 2 engine cowling doors with empty a former in the foreground at Woodford. (Hawker Siddeley Aviation Ltd via R. L. Ward Collection)

Nimrod port and starboard jet pipe fairings being hand crafted at Woodford. (Hawker Siddeley Aviation Ltd via R. L. Ward Collection)

Right: The Nimrod's large, distinctive fibreglass forward fairing, which protected the aircraft's EMI ASV-21D surveillance radar. (Hawker Siddeley Aviation Ltd via R. L. Ward Collection)

Below: The Nimrod's distinctive 'double-bubble' fuselage takes shape on the Nimrod MR.1 production line at Woodford with tailplane sections in the foreground. (Hawker Siddeley Aviation Ltd via R. L. Ward Collection)

Left: A very busy shop floor at Woodford with Nimrod production in full swing. (Hawker Siddeley Aviation Ltd via R. L. Ward Collection)

Below: The initial batch of thirty-eight Nimrod MR.1s progresses through the Woodford production line. (Hawker Siddeley Aviation Ltd via R. L. Ward Collection)

No time to stand still for the camera on the Woodford production line as another Nimrod MR.1 approaches completion. (Hawker Siddeley via G. Ashcroft)

Port intake details of an early production Nimrod MR.1 at Woodford. (Hawker Siddeley Aviation Ltd (P1-1-58) via R. L. Ward Collection)

There is no hiding the de Havilland Comet's origins on the flight deck of this Nimrod MR.2.

sonic system operators and an ESM/MAD operator. Regular navigation is performed using a Decca Doppler radar and Sperry gyrocompass, the aircraft's location being displayed on a larger than normal Ferranti RDD.

In the event of an operation that involved an attack on a surface vessel, underwing pylons could be installed outboard of the undercarriage bay. Each pylon could be fitted with a twin carrier for the AS.12 wire-guided missile; the plan was to use the AS.11 for training purposes. Also, the larger and more powerful Martel was also cleared for operational use but in the end none of them were ever deployed. Extensive trials were carried out at the A&AEE with XV148 serving as the host between March and November 1971. Another alternative, and certainly lesser known, role for the Nimrod MR.1 was as a troop-transport; forty-five troops with full kit could be carried, or fifty-five with less equipment.

Flight Testing and Trials

The flight test programme for the Nimrod began almost immediately after the maiden flight of XV148 in May 1967. Jimmy Harrison was the lead pilot during the early flight trials of both XV147 and XV148, both aircraft being installed with a plethora of instrumentation. Parachutes were worn by all of the flight test crew during the early stages, which included aerodynamic handling, asymmetric flight and engine re-lights. The bulk of the tests produced the same data as the earlier Comet trials with the exception of directional and lateral stability, which resulted in the changed design of the fin mentioned earlier. XV148 was transferred to the A&AEE operating out of Boscombe Down between May and September 1968 for assessment trials, and from October 1969 until March 1970 took part in missile trials. Tropical trials with the A&AEE were performed between July and October 1969 and between March 1970 and January 1973 and the aircraft took part in AS.11, AS.12 and Martel trials, again with the A&AEE. XV147 carried out research and development trials for the original MR.1 and MR.2 right up to its retirement and subsequent scrapping at Woodford in 2003.

The first production aircraft was Nimrod MR.1 XV226, which first flew on 28 June 1968. Fully fitted out with operational equipment, the aircraft was used for tropical and cold weather trials during 1969 and 1970. The aircraft was also used for autopilot development before it entered RAF service in January 1973. XV227 was used for armament development trials out of Woodford and Boscombe Down before entering RAF service. The aircraft was fitted with fatigue recording equipment, which it retained during its entire RAF service. XV228 initially served the A&AEE, the aircraft being used to assess navigation and tactical systems. It was also used for weapons systems trials at AUTEC in the Bahamas before entering RAF service in June 1973. XV229 was first used to clear all of the communication systems but later became one of the A&AEE's own. The aircraft was also used for SARBE personal locater beacon trials and, before entering RAF service in 1979, was fully converted to MR.2 standard.

The prototype Nimrod XV148 spent its entire career carrying out trials with the A&AEE, HAS/BAe, RRE and RSRE before it was scrapped in the early 1990s. (Hawker Siddeley Aviation Ltd via R. L. Ward Collection)

Above: XV148 captured at A&AEE Boscombe Down during Martel missile trials at Boscombe Down on 19 March 1971. (J. D. R. Rawlings via R. L. Ward Collection)

Below: Close up of an Anglo-French Martel ARM (Anti-Radiation Missile) mounted on a pylon under the wing of XV148. The missile was used operational by the Hawker Siddeley Buccaneer. (J. D. R. Rawlings via R. L. Ward Collection)

Above: The first production Nimrod MR.1, XV226, in 1968. (Hawker Siddeley Aviation Ltd (A13-1-51) via R. L. Ward Collection)

Below: Nimrod MR.1 XV226 on display at SBAC Farnborough on 20 September 1968. (R. L. Ward)

Above: Nimrod MR.1 XV299 striking a pose at SBAC Farnborough in September 1972. (R. L. Ward)

Below: A Nimrod MR.1 undergoes icing trials with the A&AEE out of Boscombe Down in company with a Canberra B.2 (Mod), WV787, and Argosy C.1 XN817. (A. J. Sheppard)

Into Service

It was on 2 October 1969 that the AOC-in-C Coastal Command, Air Marshal Sir John Lapsley, took delivery of the RAF's very first Nimrod MR.1, XV230, at a ceremony at Woodford. Later the same day, an RAF crew flew XV230 to its first home at RAF St Mawgan, to serve with MOTU (redesignated as No. 236 OCU on 1 July 1970). At least half a dozen Nimrod MR.1s were delivered to MOTU, whose primary role was to train maritime reconnaissance crews. By the time the first operational squadron began to receive the MR.1, RAF Coastal Command was no more, having been dissolved into Strike Command on 27 November 1969. No. 201 Squadron, under the command of Wg Cdr G. A. Chesworth DFC, which reformed at St Mawgan with the Shackleton MR.3 in October 1958, would be the first operational unit to receive the Nimrod MR.1, in July 1970 at RAF Kinloss. Another old Shackleton unit, No. 206 Squadron, under the command of Wg Cdr J. Wild, was the next to receive its first Nimrod MR.1s, in August 1970, also at Kinloss. No. 120 Squadron, again at Kinloss, was another long-serving maritime unit which began to replace its Shackleton MR.3s with the MR.1 from October 1970. No. 42 Squadron at St Mawgan received its first Nimrod MR.1 in April 1971 and finally, No. 203 Squadron, based at Luqa, received its first new Nimrod in October 1971. What is worth noting is that all of these units were operating the Shackleton MR.3, despite the initial requirement to re-equip Shackleton MR.2 units, which by now had already been retired.

The Nimrod MR.1 served the RAF well, the type being involved in no major accidents or incidents during its entire service, which came to an end with No. 42 Squadron, still at St Mawgan, on June 1984. However, this 'interim' aircraft had more than done its duty and it was now time for the RAF to equip with a new variant of the Nimrod, the MR.2, and a well-timed introduction it would prove to be.

Brand new Nimrod MR.1s are lined up at Woodford prior to their acceptance by the RAF in October 1969. (Hawker Siddeley Aviation Ltd via R. L. Ward Collection)

Above: The first production aircraft, Nimrod MR.1 XV226, is rolled out for the first time at Woodford on 4 September 1968. (Sport & General via R. L. Ward Collection)

Below: Nimrod MR.1 XV230, in service with No. 236 OCU, escorting the SS *Great Britain*, which is being carried by the submersible pontoon *Mulus III*, in 1970. (Via R. L. Ward Collection)

Above: Nimrod MR.1 XV230 in service with No. 42 Squadron during a display at Greenham Common on 6 July 1974. (R. L. Ward)

Below: No. 236 OCU Hawker Siddeley Nimrod MR.1 XV233 not long after entering RAF service. (Author's collection via J. D. Transport Collectables)

Above: Nimrod MR.1 XV248 climbs out of RAF Kinloss in 1973. (MOD CC PRB 2017-1 via R. L. Ward Collection)

Below: One of five Nimrod MR.1s on the static line at the RAF Finningley Silver Jubilee Review was XV257, captured on 20 July 1977. Five more performed a 'Maritime Formation' in company with Phantoms and Buccaneers. (R. L. Ward)

Above: Kinloss wing Nimrod MR.1 XZ280 '80' on final approach into RAF Kinloss. (R. L. Ward)

Below: A Nimrod MR.1 at work over the open sea intercepting a Soviet Moskva class helicopter carrier. (Hawker Siddeley via G. Ashcroft)

Left: A pristine Nimrod MR.1, XV241, about to carry out a display at the SBAC Farnborough in 1970. (R. L. Ward)

Below: A lovely study of Nimrod MR.2 XV245 prior to the hemp colour scheme being applied *c.* 1982. (Hawker Siddeley Aviation via G. Ashcroft)

Right: Nimrod MR.1 XV247 when in service with the Kinloss Wing in the late 1960s and early 1970s. The aircraft was later converted to MR.2 standard, then again to MRA.4 standard, and re-serialled ZJ516. (Hawker Siddeley Aviation via G. Ashcroft)

Below: An impressive Nimrod MR.1 four-ship flypast during the RAF Finningley Silver Jubilee Review in July 1977. (R. L. Ward)

The R.1

First formed on 15 May 1916 at Norwich with the BE.2C and BE.12, No. 51 Squadron's first operational role was Home Defence, specifically to help combat the Zeppelin threat. Operating from various aerodromes across East Anglia, the unit disbanded on 13 June 1919. No. 51 Squadron reformed at RAF Driffield on 5 March 1937 as a bomber unit and it served with Bomber Command until immediately after the Second World War, when it briefly served with Transport Command before being disbanded for a second time on 13 October 1950. On 21 August 1958 the unit was reborn again when No. 192 Squadron was renumbered to No. 51 Squadron. Stationed at RAF Watton in Norfolk, the unit now operated in the 'Special Duties' role with the Canberra B.2 and B.6 and the lead into our connection with this unit, the de Havilland Comet R.2. The latter aircraft lent itself well to the ELINT, COMINT and SIGINT roles and proved to be able to consume a large amount of clandestine equipment. Without doubt the role the Comet now found itself in would have influenced the selection of the Nimrod as the logical successor. However, it is ironic that a variant of the Boeing 707, aka the RC-135, was an option but the Nimrod would prove cheaper. As many will know, the Nimrod was succeeded by, yes, you guessed it, a US-built RC-135W!

The successors to No. 51 Squadron's three Comet R.2s were to be three Nimrod R.1s, ordered in 1969 and initially designated as the HS.801R. The cost of developing these three specially configured aircraft was to be approximately £2.38 million, with production running around £11 million. Extra special equipment would cost a further £1.25 million while extra COMINT kit, such as magnetic tape recorders, an aerial distribution system, an auto voice indicator, TR.1986/1987 and R216 receiver replacements, added an extra £545,000.

The three aircraft were delivered to RAF Wyton, the unit's home since March 1963, between July 1971 and August 1972. These aircraft contained no operational equipment whatsoever, and externally, during their early years at least, only differed from a standard MR.1 by not having a MAD boom in the tail. Other more discreet external modifications saw radomes installed in the front of each external fuel tank under the outer wings and a similar installation at the rear of the aircraft. Aerials of varying design were prevalent along the spine of the fuselage and, just like their maritime cousins, the R.1s were later upgraded with ESM Loran pods on the wingtips, a ventral fin below the rear fuselage and finlets extending above and below the tailplane to compensate for a refuelling probe, installed around 1983 (designated R.1P from then on), which was another external addition added to the small R.1 fleet.

Internally was a different matter; with the exception of the flight deck, the R.1s were completely different to their MR.1 cousins. The flight crew consisted of five, made up of two pilots, two navigators and a flight engineer, although additional space was made for a further two flight crew for extra-long sorties. Accurate navigation was crucial and the R.1 was kitted out with AD360 ADF, AD260 VOR/ILS, AN/ARN-172 TACAN, AN/ARA-50 UFH DF, LORAN and a Kollsman periscope sextant. The MR.1's ASV-21D radar was kept in place, complete with a 32-in. diameter dish, although an antenna up to five feet in size could be installed. The main cabin could accommodate up to twenty-three SIGINT crew, operating thirteen side-facing consoles. Consoles Nos 1–5 were positioned on the port side of the cabin while Nos 6–13 were on the starboard.

The R.1s were upgraded from 1980, the biggest change being the replacement of the radar with an ECKO 290 weather radar. As a result, the radar navigator's position was removed from the cockpit and the workload of the remaining navigator remained manageable thanks to removal of one of the LORAN sets, which was replaced by a Delco AN/ASN-119 Carousel IVA INS. This saw the removal of one of the external LORAN aerials, although further aerials appeared which were believed to be for direction finding. The R.1 gained the same 'Yellow Gate' ESM pods that were being fitted to the MR.2 and refuelling probes in response to Operation Corporate, although these did not appear until after the end of the Falklands War. As a result of the probe, a large ventral fin, vortex generators and tailplane finlets were fitted to all three R.1s. Underwing pylons were also brought into use, complete with modified BOZ pods which contained towed radar decoys.

Continually changing and being upgraded to keep pace with technology, the inside of the R.1 was only properly revealed after their retirement in 2011. However, we can surmise that the 1970s and 1980s were an analogue age while the 1990s and beyond have been digital, and this would have been reflected in the size and power of the equipment being used. The number of crew increased over the years as well and by the end, up to twenty-nine, including the flight crew, would have been employed on an operational sortie.

The last Comet R.2 was withdrawn from service in July 1975, leaving No. 51 Squadron with just the three Nimrod R.1s on strength; these were serialled XW664, XW665 and XW666. XW664 was first delivered to Wyton on 7 July 1971 and was destined to take more than two years to be fully kitted out. With Flt Lt G. Lambert at the controls, the first training flight was carried out 21 October 1973 and the first operational sortie on 3 May 1974, although the type was not formally commissioned into RAF service until seven days later.

All three aircraft performed faultlessly for over twenty years until 16 May 1995. XW666 had just completed a major overhaul at Kinloss and before returning to Wyton, a flight test was carried out. Not long after take-off, a fire started in engine four, closely followed by a second fire in number three engine. The pilot, Flt Lt Art Stacey, immediately turned back to base but the structure and outer panels around the engines were quickly breaking up, giving him no choice but to ditch in the Moray Firth. Stacey carried out the ditching perfectly without injury to the seven crew onboard; XW666's career, however, was undoubtedly over.

Around this time the small R.1 fleet was going through another modification programme, named 'Starwindow'. The main thrust of the programme was to re-equip the R.1s with a SIGINT suite similar to the system used by the USAF's RC-135 Rivet Joint, known as 'Open Systems'. Starwindow was made up of a pair of high-speed search receivers, wide band digital DFS and twenty-two pooled digital intercept receivers, which resulted in additional stations in the cabin. On top of this a new Special Signals package was installed, complete with a digital recording and playback suite, not to mention a pulse-signal processing capability and digital data demodulator with multi-channels. Starwindow was believed to have been further optimised in the late 1990s by additional equipment under the name 'Extract'.

No. 51 Squadron's operational commitments call for three aircraft so a replacement for XW666 was needed quickly. Nimrod MR.2 XV249, which was in store at Kinloss, was chosen for conversion to R.1P standard, the work being carried out at Woodford under the codename 'Project Anneka'. The latter was named after Anneka Rice's *Challenge Anneka*, which was axed by the BBC in 1995! Conversion work took from 13 October 1995 until 19 December 1996, when XV249 was delivered to RAF Waddington, the new home of No. 51 Squadron since April 1995. It was at Waddington that the sensitive equipment was installed (including Starwindow), a task that took nearly four months to complete, the aircraft returning to the air on 11 April 1997. On 27 October 2009, XW665 made its final flight, leaving XW664 and XV249 to soldier on until the end. This came on 28 June 2011 for XV249 and 12 July 2011 for XW664, both aircraft being preserved intact at the RAF Museum, Cosford, and East Midlands Aeropark respectively. The cockpit sections of both XW665 and XW666 both survive as well – the former at the Auto & Technik Museum, Sinsheim, and the latter at the South Yorkshire Aircraft Museum, Doncaster.

Above: No. 51 Squadron Nimrod R.1 XW664, *c.* 1991, at the time of the seventy-fifth anniversary of the unit. (R. L. Ward)

Below: Another view of No. 51 Squadron's Nimrod R.1 XW664 at RAF Wyton on 24 October 1991. (R. L. Ward)

Above: Air-to-air imagery, let alone ground shots, of No. 51 Squadron aircraft was pretty rare prior to the 1990s. This image of Nimrod R.1 XW665 was a treat back in the early 1990s. (Crown Copyright via C. Hearn)

Below: No. 51 Squadron Nimrod R.1 XW665 in the foreground and XW644 in the background banking away. (Crown Copyright via C. Hearn)

No. 51 Squadron
Nimrod R.1 XW666
taxiing out for
take-off at RAF
Wyton, *c.* 1984.
(R. L. Ward)

A No. 51 Squadron
Nimrod R.1
pictured on 16 May
1995. Two weeks
later the aircraft
was successfully
ditched 4½ miles
north-east of
Lossiemouth.
(Via R. L. Ward
Collection)

An impressive
air-to-air study of
No. 51 Squadron
Nimrod R.1 XW665
after relocating
from RAF Wyton to
RAF Waddington.
The Nimrod is
accompanied by
a No. 8 Squadron
E-3D Sentry and
a No. 5 Squadron
Sentinel R.1 ASTOR
(Airborne Stand-Off
Radar). (Crown
Copyright via
C. Hearn)

The MR.2

The Nimrod MR.1 had impressed Strike Command and as a result a further eight aircraft (XZ280 to XZ287 (Contract KA/2B/38)) were ordered in January 1972, delivery being expected by 1975, a date that would slip by a few years. In the end, only five of this batch were delivered as MR.1s, the remainder becoming other variants or being placed into storage at Kinloss, their fate being covered later.

Not long after, or maybe even before, the Nimrod MR.1 entered service, thoughts were already being directed towards the aircraft's replacement. The acceptance by the RAF of the MR.1 as an 'interim' aircraft would soon be addressed with a new, upgraded variant, simply designated the Nimrod MR.2. The main thrust of the upgrade was to replace the MR.1's dated analogue systems with modern digital systems, revolving around a Central Tactical System (CTS). The obsolete ASV 21 radar was replaced with the Searchwater radar, a GEC-Marconi AQS-901 acoustic processer designed to work with modern sonobouys, a Hanbush mission date recorder and ESM ('Yellow Gate') in wing tip pods were installed, although the latter was not a common site on the MR.2 until 1985. The Searchwater radar, developed by Thorn EMI, was a maritime surveillance radar capable of carrying out anti-submarine and anti-surface duties. It had its own data-processing sub-system and could operate at very long range in the worst of sea conditions. The Searchwater radar installed in the Nimrod MR.2 was the first of a series which was continually developed over the years and installed in a wide range of maritime aircraft, including the final piece in our story, the Nimrod MRA.4. The AQS-901 could analyse and classify contacts using passive and active sonobouys while the CTS included a Ferranti FIN 1012 INS for short-range navigation and Omega for long-range. Together, all of these systems made the Nimrod MR.2 one of the most potent and powerful maritime reconnaissance in the world.

The original MR.1 was effectively gutted of its dated electronics and refurnished with a modern suite. Thirty-one airframes with the lowest hours were initially chosen for conversion to MR.2 standard. Whilst this work was being carried out, Hawker Siddeley took a serious look at an airborne early warning (AEW) version of the Nimrod for the first time, designed to take over the role from the Shackleton AEW.2, which was using a radar system from the retired Fairey Gannet AEW.3. Unfortunately, the ideas remained on paper; the time for the Nimrod to be converted to this role would come, but not just yet.

The second prototype, Nimrod XV147, was chosen to be fitted out with the full MR.2 suite of new systems. XV147 first flew with the MR.2 systems on board on 15 April 1977 and was later joined by a further three MR.1 to MR.2 conversions, taking part in a comprehensive development programme which racked up more than 1,000 flying hours between the four aircraft. The first production MR.2, XV236, made its maiden flight on 13 February 1979, by which time Hawker Siddeley had merged with BAC to become British Aerospace.

XV236 was transferred to RAF charge on 23 August 1979 while No. 206 Squadron at Kinloss became the first operational unit to convert to the MR.2. Sadly though, tragedy struck early when on 17 November 1980, during conversion training, Nimrod MR.2 XV256 crashed a mere 800 yards off the end of Kinloss main runway 07. Immediately after take-off, the aircraft suffered a huge bird strike which damaged three out of four engines, leaving the aircraft in a perilous situation. The captain, Flt Lt N. W. Anthony RAAF, and co-pilot, Fg Off S. P. Belcher, had no other choice than to keep the aircraft level and settle it down on the top of the young, soft pine trees in Roseisle Forest at minimum speed. Miraculously, the aircraft came down in one piece and eighteen crew members survived, despite the aircraft catching fire immediately. However, both Anthony and Belcher lost their lives and because of their skilful actions in saving their crew, Flt Lt Anthony was posthumously awarded the AFC while Fg Off Belcher was posthumously awarded the Queen's Commendation for Brave Conduct. The aircraft carved a swathe through Roseisle Forest that was over 300 metres long, evidence of which can still be seen today.

The conversion programme continued unabated with newly converted Nimrod MR.2s leaving Woodfood in a new hemp upper colour and grey lower surfaces colour scheme. The final MR.2 was delivered on 19 December 1985. Only one aircraft was built as a 'new' MR.2; this was XZ284, which had been in storage as an incomplete airframe. In the meantime, Nimrod MR.2 XV227 was furnished with a suite of instruments so it could take part in the Nimrod Operational Load Measurement Programme. XV227 arrived at Kinloss on 2 December 1981, beginning its operational service with the Kinloss and St Mawgan wing. All of the information gathered by the plethora of instruments on board was gathered and collated at Woodford and used for the continuing modification of the Nimrod fleet.

XV241, a Nimrod MR.1 was also used in support of the MR.2 modifications, the machine serving as a development aircraft focussing on the ECM fit on top of the fin, which was to be replaced by a new Loran ESM. Arriving at Woodford in May 1978, XV241 was gutted and given a major overhaul. All ECM equipment was taken out and empty ESM pods were fitted to the wingtips; the original ECM housing on top of the fin was left in place to maintain the aerodynamics of the aircraft. In this new guise, XV241 first flew in September 1979 and flight trials began to determine the final design of the wingtip pods. When this was achieved the new pods were installed on the Nimrod R.1s first, while XV241 was converted to MR.2 standard in November 1982. XV241 continued to carry out a number of ESM trials out of Woodford before it was returned to RAF in August 1986.

The hard-working prototype XV148 also contributed to the MR.2 programme when it was transferred from Woodford to Bedford. Here its nose and tail were removed and MR.2 wing hard points were fitted, the remnants of the aircraft continuing to serve as a test rig for a further ten years.

Kinloss Wing Nimrod MR.2 XV236, c. 1981. This was the first MR.2 to enter operational service with the RAF. (Via R. L. Ward Collection)

Above: XV236 enjoyed a long and trouble-free career which concluded in 2008. The aircraft is pictured in service with No. 42 Squadron, during a display at Farnborough on 14 September 1998. (R. L. Ward)

Below: An early example of an MR.2 is this nice low-level air-to-air of XV228 over the Moray Firth on 27 July 1981, then in service with No. 206 Squadron. (Via R. L. Ward Collection)

Above: The only 'new' Nimrod MR.2 to be delivered to the RAF was XZ284. Here the aircraft is pictured in service with No. 206 Squadron during a performance at the Mildenhall Air Show on 24 May 1997. (R. L. Ward)

Below: Nimrod MR.2 XV241 in service with the A&AEE, *c.* 1985. (R. L. Ward)

Above: Another long serving example was Nimrod MR.2 XV247, seen here in service with No. 201 Squadron. (Crown Copyright via Chris Hearn)

Below: An impressive Nimrod four-ship made up of Kinloss Wing aircraft. (Crown Copyright via Chris Hearn)

Above: After carrying out extensive trials, XV241 returned to operational service with the RAF from 1986 until 2010. (Crown Copyright via C. Hearn)

Below left: The last example of the Nimrod MR.2 to serve at RAF Kinloss was XV244 and, appropriately, the aircraft is still there on display to this day. (BAE Systems via R. L. Ward Collection)

Below right: An unknown Nimrod MR.2 clings on to the remnants of the day before returning home to RAF Kinloss. (British Aerospace via J. A. 'Robby' Robinson)

Airborne Early Warning

On 1 January 1972, ex-Hawker Hunter unit No. 8 Squadron was reformed at RAF Kinloss, equipped with the Avro Shackleton AEW.2. Converted from the MR.2 variant, this AEW version of the venerable Shackleton appeared at the very end of the service career of the MR variant and few would have predicted that it would extend the type's RAF service by nearly two decades. The AEW.2 was, like the early Nimrods that entered service only a few years before, meant to be an interim.

By the mid-1970s the final remnants of the British aviation industry – BAC (British Aircraft Corporation), Hawker Siddeley and Scottish Aviation – merged into one major group called British Aerospace (BAe), which was founded on 29 April 1977. Not long after, a replacement for the hard-working Shackleton AEW.2 was considered and the Nimrod was the lead candidate for taking over the role. Once again it would be a Comet that would kick-start the project, this time in the shape of Comet 4C XW626 (Ex-G-APDS (Ex-BOAC)), which was already conveniently serving MinTech as a Nimrod development aircraft. Conversion work began in early 1977, the aircraft making its maiden flight in its new, rather unflattering configuration on 28 June of that year.

The design of the new AEW Nimrod, which would be given the designation AEW.3, hinged around a pair of large GEC Marconi radars contained within huge bulbous radomes positioned in the nose and tail of the aircraft. XW626 would be modified with just the large nose radar, plus a redesigned fin, and as a result was nicknamed the 'Comrod' thanks to its hybrid appearance. The lack of the balancing tail radome meant that the directional stability of the aircraft was reduced but for the 'mundane' radar tests the Comrod would be used for, this did not cause too much trouble to the Woodford test pilots, including 'Robby' Robinson, who remembers the period well:

> By the beginning of 1979 the initial radar trials on XW626 were coming to an end and the Ministry decided to reclaim the aircraft and use it for general equipment trials at RAE Bedford. XW626 had been modified for the radar trials by putting a large radome on the nose, without the balancing tail radome due to go on the production aircraft. This meant that its directional stability was reduced, rather like a dart with too small flights. This had been fairly unimportant during our mundane radar tests when the aircraft had been flown exclusively by company test pilots but handing over to the RAE was another story. It would need some sort of official clearance and this would entail some basic handling tests to establish the flight envelope, albeit a very restricted one. I was given this job and the first tests were to be rolling characteristics. This seemed to be a simple enough task.
>
> On 23 April, Dave Pearson and I briefed to carry out the first handling flight, I queried whether the rolls were to be with or without rudder assistance and received a woolly sort of an answer from the Flight Test department, l gathered that it was rather up to me. It would be preferable if

it could meet the requirements without rudder but if I had to I could use it. The first part of the flight was without incident. Rolls with restricted aileron deflection were fine and we were ready to move on to rolls with full aileron. It should be explained that every aircraft has a side-slip angle limit over which the fin is likely to snap off (like on an early Victor), or at least become very over stressed. XW626, basically a Comet 4C, had a limit of 17° at low speed and I was very conscious of this.

XW626, in its part Nimrod AEW configuration, made its first flight from Woodford on 26 June 1977. Emblazed with the words 'Radar AEW Trials' and 'British Aerospace – Marconi Avionics' along the fuselage, the aircraft was quite a head turner. Unlike the Boeing E-3 AWAC, which the US government were very keen for the MoD to buy, the Nimrod AEW.3's two large Marconi radars gave 180° coverage apiece, in effect giving a complete, uninterrupted 360° coverage. The system was far from perfect at this stage but when it worked, it was certainly a world-beating configuration, though pressure put on British Aerospace, and in particular Marconi, would take its toll.

The MoD placed an order for eleven Nimrod AEW.3s, all of which would be converted from current Nimrod MR airframes. The aircraft chosen were XV259, XV261, XV262, XV263, XZ280–283 and XZ285–287; of this batch, with the exception of XZ285–287, all were ex-MR.1 airframes, the latter batch of three being built as MR.2s. Three aircraft were chosen as Development Batch aircraft; these were XZ286 (DB.1), XZ287 (DB.2) and XZ281 (DB.3), DB.1 taking to the air for the first time as a Nimrod AEW.3 on 16 July 1980 with Charles Masefield at the controls. This event was witnessed by more than 2,000 British Aerospace employees and once airborne, the prototype Nimrod XV148 acted as a chase plane for this historic event. Used for nothing more than airframe and handling tests, DB.1 did not contain any of the complex equipment needed for the AEW role but this did not stop the aircraft being showcased at the Farnborough Air Show, an event in which it was displayed every day.

Both prototypes XZ287 (DB.2) and XZ281 (DB.3) were completed as per an operational AEW.3, complete with the core of the aircraft, the MSA (mission system avionics). The MSA was installed into both aircraft at Hatfield by Marconi-Elliot (shortly to become GEC Avionics) along with all radar equipment. The MSA was controlled by a GEC 4080M computer which was designed to handle all the data provided by the two radar scanners, an IFF, an ESM system and the inertial navigation system. As powerful as the GEC computer was for the day, it struggled from the outset to cope with the amount of data it received. On top of this problem, when both radar scanners and all of the on-board electronics were running simultaneously, an enormous amount of heat was generated. To help solve this problem, extra fuel tanks which had been placed in the now unused weapons bay were used as large heat exchangers to keep the electronics cool. This extra tankage also had the added advantage of increasing the aircraft's range by some margin; however, it was discovered that the cooling effect only worked when the tanks were at least half full.

Both XZ287 (DB.2) and XZ281 (DB.3) would begin their test programmes out of Hatfield while XV286 (DB.1) was put through its paces with the A&AEE at Boscombe Down. Once all trials had been completed, the plan was that all three aircraft would return to Woodford, where they would be brought up to production and prepared for delivery to the RAF.

Events were destined not to go according to plan in a big, expensive way for Marconi at least. The radar was incredibly advanced and complicated, not helped by a changing remit from the customer, who called for much more from the radar system than was originally requested. As these changes were introduced, costs began to spiral, complicated by a restless workforce at Woodford who were intent on industrial action.

The AEW programme as a whole had slipped two years behind schedule and the planned entry in service date of 1984 was looking doubtful. Problems with sub-contractors contributed to the delays and crucial items like racking for the mission equipment meant that XZ286 had to fly with important avionics not present. By late 1984, XZ286 was fully equipped and was delivered to RAF Waddington on 18 December. The station had been fully prepared for the arrival of the new aircraft; engineering and maintenance hangars had been modified or built and flight simulators had been installed. Before the Nimrod AEW.3 could be cleared for operational service, it would have to pass through the TEU (Trials Evaluation Unit). Sadly, all did not go well and in the end only three examples of the aircraft were delivered to Waddington. 'Robby' Robinson remembers working with the TEU and the unfortunate outcome:

In 1985 a team of RAF specialists joined us. Their task was to assess the system and report on its progress to their masters. I think perhaps that their masters had a separate agenda. The members of the team were nice blokes, entering into the social side of the company with enthusiasm, becoming regular attendees at our Lancaster Club and giving their own parties at the house they had rented in Stockport. They were all aircrew so they integrated with the trials team very easily. They gave us no problems although I think that the Marconi men began to feel uneasy. It must have been difficult to carry out development tests with someone looking over their shoulders and reporting every little hitch (which are inevitable in any trials) to higher-ups who were intent on seeing the system fail. As time went by it became obvious that the project was in trouble politically and it culminated with a flight on the 18 November 1986.

I was told that the Secretary of State for Defence, Mr George Younger, was coming to fly with us to see how things were going. It was obvious that this was a political visit, not idle curiosity. Mr. Younger could not be expected to understand the technical aspects of the system and his presence, I surmised, was so that he could say truthfully that he had observed it in action before making a decision on its viability. I met Mr Younger at the briefing, took him aboard and sat him on the jump seat behind me. He was extremely pleasant, taking a great interest in our preparations for flight but keeping out of the way. The take off and climb went without a hitch and when we reached our patrol station the Squadron Leader in charge of the RAF team led him back to observe the demonstration. I am not sure that the RAF men ever knew that I could listen in to their private intercom but I could and I heard them talking to the Minister and subtly denigrating the performance of the system with remarks such as "You see Sir, there is the problem we spoke about." Eventually the demonstration was over and Mr Younger came back to the flight deck and we returned to base where, after landing, I presented him with a company AEW tie. He changed from his borrowed flying suit and climbed into his car and left. He did not attend the debriefing, neither did the RAF team. The next week it was announced that the project was cancelled and that the Air Force would be getting the AWACS that it had wanted all along.

Although we were sorry that the project had been cancelled we of BAe were not too upset. It is never nice to be associated with a failure but we had delivered, on schedule, all six airframes to RAF Waddington where they were to be fitted out with the Marconi electronics. So we had been paid our money. It was a different case for Marconi.

The fate of the Nimrod AEW.3 was sealed. Costs continued to rise and on 18 December 1986 the programme was cancelled. The bulk of the airworthy airframes were flown to RAF Abingdon, where they languished for a few years before being scrapped. Only XV263 saw some kind of RAF service when it was flown to RAF Finningley to serve as an instructional airframe. In serial order the aircraft were disposed of as follows. XV259 was broken up at Stock, Essex, in late 1998 although the fuselage did survive for some time while the nose, the only piece of an AEW.3 to survive, is preserved at the Solway Aviation Museum, Carlisle. XV261 (8968M) was scrapped at RAF Lyneham in 1995; XV262 was scrapped at Abingdon in 1992; XV263 (8967M), scrapped in 2002; XZ280 and XZ281 were both scrapped at Abingdon during 1991 and 1992 while XZ282 (9000M) was scrapped at Elgin in early 1996, presumably having been stored at RAF Kinloss for a time. XZ283, XZ285, XZ286 and XZ287 were all scrapped at RAF Abingdon in 1991/92 although the rear section of XZ286 (8968M) was transferred to RAF Kinloss for GI duties.

The MoD turned their attention to the Boeing E-3 Sentry instead and placed an order for seven aircraft to be delivered to the RAF in 1990. Serialled ZH101 to ZH107, the first aircraft, designated as the Sentry AEW.1, arrived at RAF Waddington on 26 March 1991 and continue to serve to this day.

Comet 4C XW626, following an extensive facelift for the Nimrod AEW.3 trials, arrives at Farnborough in 1978 with 'Robby' Robinson and Charles Masefield at the controls. (Via 'Robby' Robinson)

De Havilland Comet 4 XW626, the Nimrod AEW trials aircraft. (Via R. L. Ward Collection)

Above and right: Nimrod AEW.2 XZ286 (DB.1) on roll-out day at Woodford on 20 April 1980. (R. L. Ward)

Above: The maiden flight of Nimrod AEW.3 XZ286 (DB.1) with Charles Masefield and Jonny Cruse at the controls. (British Aerospace via Harry Holmes)

Below: Nimrod AEW.3 XZ286 puts on a fine display at Abingdon on 12 September 1981. (R. L. Ward)

Above: Nimrod AEW.3 XZ281 (DB.3) during the type's mission systems flight programme on 24 November 1982. (British Aerospace via Harry Holmes)

Below: Whatever your thoughts on the appearance of the Nimrod AEW.3, it was certainly an aircraft that struck a dramatic pose in flight. (British Aerospace via Harry Holmes)

Above: This was as close as the Nimrod AEW.3 came to entering RAF service; this is a view of three examples at RAF Waddington. (British Aerospace via Harry Holmes)

Below: Nimrod AEW.3 XZ286 being dismantled at RAF Abingdon. (R. L. Ward)

Above: Nimrod AEW.3 XZ285 under the charge of the AEWTU at RAF Waddington on 1 June 1985. (R. L. Ward)

Below: A sad end for the AEW.3 fleet, the bulk of which ended up at RAF Abingdon. XZ287 (DB.2) is in the centre and, along with its colleagues, was scrapped during 1991 and 1992.

The last Hurrah! The MRA.4

Despite the fact that the Nimrod MR.2 was one of, if not the best maritime patrol aircraft in the world, by the early 1990s it was clear that the type could not go on forever and a replacement would be needed for the RAF of the twenty-first century. The MoD issued Staff Requirement (Air) SRA 420 in 1993, which called for a 'Replacement Maritime Patrol Aircraft' for the Nimrod MR.2. The MoD also required that a production order for the new aircraft be placed by 1995/1996; the scene was set for another scenario destined to cost the British taxpayer dear.

The MoD's requirement was made available to world's aircraft manufacturers, including Bréguet, who presented a revamped version of the twin-engined Atlantique; Lockheed-Martin with the Orion 2000; and Lockheed Tactical Systems UK (Ex-Loral), who offered their own version of the Orion. These were both aircraft types which were on the table back in the 1960s. BAe Systems did not, on initial inspection, offer a design but instead produced a completed upgraded version of the MR.2, initially named the Nimrod 2000. After studying all of the proposals, the Atlantique was dismissed at an early stage due to a lack of engines and both Orion designs fell by the wayside, leaving the Nimrod 2000 as the winner, most likely because it was by far the cheapest option and the defence cuts of the 1990s were taking their toll.

The Nimrod 2000 would still resemble the Nimrod thanks to the use of the original fuselage but would feature new wings, engines, undercarriage, a glass cockpit and, of course, a completely new suite of avionics. Thanks to the destruction of the original Nimrod jigs many years earlier, new airframes were not on the cards, so instead the lowest hour Nimrod MR.2 airframes were selected for conversion.

In December 1996 it was announced that the MoD had awarded BAe Systems a £2.4 billion contract for twenty-one Nimrod 2000 aircraft, which by now had been renamed the Nimrod MRA.4 (Maritime Reconnaissance and Attack Mk.4). Working with Airbus, the aircraft's new wing had a span 12 feet longer and had an area 23 per cent larger than the original MR.2. Four underwing hardpoints added great versatility, enabling the MRA.4 to carry a variety of weapons, including ASRAAM, ATARM, Harpoon, Maverick, SLAM-ER and Storm Shadow. With a much higher all-up weight, the MRA.4 needed more power and new engines as the Rolls-Royce Spey could not be developed any further. The Rolls-Royce BR710 high-bypass turbofan was selected, capable of delivering 15,500 lbs of thrust. A highly efficient engine which used 30 per cent less fuel than the Spey and produced 25 per cent more thrust, the main design influence the new engines would have on the aircraft was much larger intakes; 50 per cent larger than the MR.2's.

Internally, the Nimrod MRA.4 was unrecognisable from its predecessor. A fibre-optic tactical command system (TCS), a development of Boeing's TMS-2000 system, was connected to the MRA.4's MIL-STD 1553B databus. Incredibly powerful, the TCS was a display programme which handled data distribution, dispersing the information to seven

50

high-resolution workstations, each of which was reconfigurable. The aircraft's sensors included the Thales Searchwater 2000MR multimode search radar which produced Doppler modes for air-to-air searches. A synthetic aperture radar could be sued for ground mapping and an inverse synthetic aperture radar served for identifying targets. The Searchwater 2000 worked as well over water as it did over land and in a single sweep could cover an area the size of the United Kingdom every ten seconds! ASW tasking was carried out using the CDC/Ultra UYS503/AQS970 acoustic processer while a Northrop Grumman electro-optical search and detection system (EOSDS), installed in a retractable ball turret under the nose, provided an advanced visual search capability.

Another impressive piece of new equipment onboard the MRA.4 was the Elta EL/L-8300UK electronic support measures (ESM) system. The powerful system could identify and classify a large range of radar equipment installed on a ship or an aircraft. Other systems included the defensive aids sub-system (DASS), which was made up of radar warning receiver (RWR), a missile approach warner, infra-red countermeasures (IRCM) and chaff dispensers. Total crew for the MRA.4 was ten, two of which were flight crew (no need for a navigator or flight engineer) while the mission crew in the rear comprised a pair of tactical co-ordinators, two acoustics operators, a communications manager, one radar operator, one ESM operator and one for all other tasking.

The in service date of the MRA.4 was now planned for 2003 but this was pushed back by two years when the fuselages were moved from Hurn up to Woodford. The first prototype, PA.1 (aka ZJ516 (ex-XV247)), was rolled out on 16 August 2004. The aircraft, in the hands of BAe Systems Chief Test Pilot John Turner, carried out its maiden flight ten days later. Accompanied by a Hawk and a Tucano, the two-hour flight was concluded at Warton, from where flight testing would be carried out. PA.1 had no mission equipment on board, however the second aircraft, PA.2 (aka ZJ518 (ex-XV234)), had a full mission system and first flew on 12 December 2004.

Nimrod MR.2 XV245 was one of twelve aircraft selected for conversion to MRA.4 standard. Unfortunately, the aircraft, having received serial ZJ522 (PA-9), was scrapped at Woodford in February 2011 before the Nimrod even reached the conversion stage. (Crown Copyright via R. L. Ward Collection)

Above: The prototype Nimrod MRA.4, ZJ516 (PA-1), being rolled out at Woodford. First flown on 26 August 2004, the aircraft made its last flight of 9 March 2010 only to be scrapped at Woodford on 15 March 2011. (BAe Systems via R. L. Ward Collection)

Below: 12 December 2004 and the second MRA.4, ZJ518 (PA-2), takes off from Woodford. This development aircraft continued flying until 5 March 2010 and was scrapped the same day as ZJ516. (BAe Systems via R. L. Ward Collection)

There were a number of features that gave away the difference between the Nimrod MR.2 and the MRA.4. One of the more obvious ones was the much larger air intakes needed for the Rolls-Royce BR.710 turbofans. (BAe Systems via R. L. Ward Collection)

Nimrod MRA.4 ZJ518 captured banking over Conwy Bay. (BAe Systems via R. L. Ward Collection)

At this point everything was looking reasonably rosy; however, in July 2006 the MoD reduced the production contract to just twelve aircraft, although this did include a thirty-year-long support contract. By spring 2009, the contract had been reduced to just nine aircraft and expected entry into service moved to 2010. Kinloss was in no doubt that the MRA.4 would arrive as a dedicated simulator and training programme was set in place, not to mention new infrastructure. In the meantime, three more MRA.4s took to the air: PA.3 (aka ZJ517 (ex-XV242)) on 29 August 2005; PA.4 (aka ZJ514 (ex-XV251)) on 10 September 2009; and PA.5 (aka ZJ515 (ex-XV258)) on 8 March 2010.

Neither Kinloss nor the RAF was destined to ever see the MRA.4 enter service. A new coalition government took over in May 2010 and one of their policies was to reduce MoD expenditure. The RAF lost its Harrier force, a number of Tornadoes and, most painful of all, the Nimrod MRA.4, which by now had racked up an eye-watering £4 billion! During January and February 2011, the aircraft were towed to the far side of Woodford and scrapped.

Operational

Cod Wars (Operations Dewey and Heliotrope)

The Cod Wars were a series of 'militarised interstate disputes', rather than a conventional war, which took place between Iceland and the United Kingdom over fishing rights in the North Atlantic. The first of three 'wars' took place from 1958 to 1961 and was supported by Shackletons from 18 Group. It was the second, which took place from 1 September 1972 until 8 November 1973, that involved the newly into service Nimrod MR.1, under the Royal Navy codename Operation Dewey. The cause of this 'Cod War' was that the Icelandic Government extended its fishing rights from a 12-mile fishery zone to a 50-mile one in an effort to conserve its own stocks and to increase the share of total catches amongst its fleet. The British objected to this but did not initially respond until the ICG cutter *Ægir* cut the warps of the British trawler *Peter Scott* (H103) on 5 September. A further eight trawlers would have their warps cut before the year was out.

The Royal Navy responded by sending the frigate HMS *Aurora* to the area and when a further incident on 18 October saw *Ægir* ramming the trawler *Aldershot*, a second frigate was committed. The ICG ships could carry a single Bell 47 helicopter and were armed with a single 47 mm and a 57 mm cannon while the British frigates were obviously well-armed and carried a single Wasp helicopter. Ironically, one of the first incidents that the Nimrod was called in to support was in response to the *Ægir*, which had radioed a distress call during a search for a missing Icelandic trawler. As the dispute continued, the Nimrods, operating from RAF Kinloss and supplied by Nos 120, 201 and 206 Squadrons, provided extra information to the Royal Navy, whose Wasp helicopters had neither the range nor endurance to cover such a large area.

By May 1973 Nimrod patrols were increased to two per day, and on occasion three, while the Royal Navy now had a minimum of three ships on patrol. By July, Britannias from Nos 99/511 Squadrons, operating from RAF Brize Norton, supplemented the Nimrods, the transport aircraft having both Nimrod aircrew and observers on board. The reason for this was that the new Nimrods were exceeding their peacetime flying hour quota, the Britannia's 10¼ hour sorties helping to alleviate this unforeseen problem. Several more close encounters between ICG gunboats and British warships occurred before the politicians sat around the table. 3 October 1973 saw the last RAF sortie flown and the Nimrod fleet returned to more routine operations.

One of the conclusions resulting from the second Cod War was that Iceland would be allowed to fish its new 50-mile fishery zone for a further two years. When this agreement ended, a third Cod War began on 15 October 1975, Iceland this time introducing a 200-mile fishery zone. Four weeks later Operation Dewey began again, and so did the warp cutting.

The RAF contribution this time came under the title Operation Heliotrope and just like the second Cod War, the Nimrod fleet began extensive patrols in the area, helping the Royal Navy to identify friend from 'foe'. Also, just like the previous 'war', the RAF was denied use of Icelandic airfields but ATC would still be provided by the airport at Keflavík. It was a slightly different picture for the RAF by this time as the Britannia was bowing out, but a contingency to use the Hercules C.1 and the Hastings T.5 was employed instead. In the end, only the Hastings was used, the aircraft having a fish symbol applied to their noses for each sortie flown, which numbered twenty out of a total of 178.

Operations were very similar to the previous dispute, the Nimrod and Hastings providing large coverage while the more capable Wessex, in company with the Wasp helicopter, helped to locate the ICG gunships. This 'war' appeared to be coming to an end quite quickly and in late January 1976, both the Royal Navy and RAF suspended their operations while politicians attempted to come up with a deal. However, talks soon failed and the number of collisions quickly increased and became more aggressive. On 11 May, the crew of the *Ægir* attempted to board the British trawler *Primella*, the latter turning on its heels in an attempt to escape the cutter, which fired several shots around the vessel. Picking up the *Primella*'s distress calls, the Royal Navy called in a patrolling Nimrod, and after threatening to attack unless the *Ægir* disengaged, the ICG vessel made the right decision and was shadowed for some time after the incident.

Despite how close a Nimrod had come to delivering its weapons for the first time in anger, the ICG vessels continued to harass British trawlers. With the Royal Navy running out of ships that had not been damaged during Operation Dewey, the third and final Cod War came to an end on 30 May 1976.

Operation Tapestry

As an island nation, the United Kingdom has a colossal amount of water to protect, which increased in 1976 when the EEC agreed to a 200-mile exclusion economic zone (EEZ). Offshore oil and gas rigs were on the increase and it was soon realised that these isolated platforms were potentially vulnerable to terrorist attack. In an effort to protect these platforms, Operation Tapestry was launched on 1 January 1977 and once again the Nimrod fleet would shoulder the burden of responsibility. The plan was simple at first: to carry out three surveillance flights per week, these flights performing two functions. These were to keep a close eye on oil and gas rigs from a structural point of view and to make contact with each rig by radio. The second function was to patrol the fishing grounds and to identify fishing trawlers that were allowed to fish in those waters. The former function was achieved via a maritime VHF radio, the Nimrod crews using the callsign 'Watchdog' to identify themselves.

Four patrol zones were established around the United Kingdom: one west of Rockall, another north of Shetland, the North Sea and the Channel and Western Approaches. When a suspicious vessel was encountered by the Nimrod crew, its position was immediately relayed to the Royal Navy's Fishery Protection Service. No. 42 Squadron and No. 236 OCU operating out of RAF St Mawgan covered the Channel and Western Approaches while the remainder was patrolled by RAF Kinloss-based squadrons. A No. 42 Squadron Nimrod carried out an aerial 'arrest' of a Spanish trawler fishing illegally in the Western Approaches in 1978. The vessel was escorted to Milford Haven. Any vessels caught discharging oil or waste into the sea were also reported by the Nimrod crews, not to mention monitoring suspicious vessels which were potentially drug running, carrying illegal immigrants or smuggling.

In August 1985, Operation Tapestry came to an end; the oil rig protection element at least was transferred from the RAF and sold out to a civilian contract. Straddling the transition of the Nimrod MR.1 to the MR.2, No. 236 OCU and Nos 42, 120, 201 and 206 Squadrons all played their part in Tapestry.

Cyprus

On 15 July 1974 the Mediterranean island of Cyprus was in crisis following a coup d'état which removed Archbishop Makarios. Just four days later the RAF was involved in the crisis when a No. 203 Squadron Nimrod, operating out of Luqa, came across forty Turkish military vessels heading towards Cyprus. Whilst keeping tabs on the force, the Nimrod was intercepted by a Turkish Air Force F-100 Super Sabre and then by F-84F Thunderstreak. However, neither posed a threat as they were in turn intercepted by the Lightings of No. 56 Squadron, operating out of RAF Akrotiri. Following the invasion of northern Cyprus by Turkish forces, the resident Vulcan squadron was withdrawn to RAF Luqa and the sea north of the island was declared a war zone, which effectively reduced the 'safe' operating area of No. 203 Squadron's Nimrods.

No. 203 Squadron continued to carry out reconnaissance flights over the island in company with No. 13 Squadron's Canberra PR.7s and PR.9s, also operating out of Luqa. One No. 203 Squadron Nimrod was involved in a SAR sortie when it responded to the crew of the Turkish destroyer *Kocatepe*, which had been sunk by its own aircraft! No. 203 Squadron's reward for its service during this period was disbandment on 31 December 1977 as part of the Labour government's White Paper, which called for a 25 per cent reduction of the Nimrod force.

Nimrod MR.1s at rest at Kinloss in between Operation Tapestry sorties. (Hawker Siddeley Aviation via G. Ashcroft)

Above: St Mawgan Wing Hawker Siddeley Nimrod MR.1 XV237, pictured at RAF St Mawgan during the early 1970s. (Via J. D. Collectables)

Below: Kinloss Wing Hawker Siddeley Nimrod MR.1 XV242 at rest during the third and final Cod War in early 1976. (Via R. L. Ward Collection)

Above: The Nimrod MR.1 saw extensive service during the second and third Cod Wars and contributed to Operation Tapestry from 1977 to February 1983. (Via R. L. Ward Collection)

Below: Busy pans at RAF Kinloss during the 1970s; visible are Nimrod MR.1s XV236, XV251 and XV262. (Hawker Siddeley Ltd (P1-1-219) via 'Bluespingo')

Above: Thanks to a lack of aerials, lumps and bumps compared to the Nimrod MR.2, the MR.1 was a much cleaner looking aircraft. (Crown Copyright via R. L. Ward Collection)

Below: No. 120 Squadron Nimrod MR.1 XV244 out of RAF Kinloss swoops low over a Soviet ocean-going tug, 100 miles north of Scotland, around August 1978. (MoD (PRB 5753-6) via R. L. Ward Collection)

Above: What a different air force we had in the later 1970s; a No. 201 Squadron Nimrod MR.1 accompanied by a pair of No. 13 Squadron Canberra PR.7s overflies a line of Lightnings. (Via R. L. Ward Collection)

Below: Nimrod MR.2 XV252 keeping tabs on what could possibly be a Soviet trawler. (Crown Copyright via R. L. Ward Collection)

The Falklands – Operation Corporate

It was 5 April 1982 when the Nimrod first contributed to events occurring 8,000 miles away in the South Atlantic. A pair of No. 42 Squadron Nimrod MR.1s, XV244 and XV258, were despatched from St Mawgan to Wideawake on Ascension Island complete with three flight crews and the minimum number of ground crew sufficient to establish a detachment. Arriving on 6 April, the aircraft were tasked with providing maritime reconnaissance and SAR cover. XV258 flew the first operation the next day in support of the Task Force which was gathering at home.

The RAF had a distinct lack of AEW cover at this time and there is no doubting that the USAF lent a hand in that department. A pair of No. 206 Squadron Nimrod MR.2s joined the Wideawake detachment but it was clear that the length of the sorties would require an air-to-air refuelling capability. It was time to approach British Aerospace for a solution and time was of the essence. British Aerospace Chief Test Pilot at that time was 'Robby' Robinson:

> On the 14 of April the Board of Directors had received a telephone call from the Ministry of Defence asking how long it would take to give the Nimrod a flight refuelling capability. As it happened Charles Masefield and I had carried out a test in 1980 to see if such a thing could be done. We flew behind a Victor tanker and, although we had no probe fitted, we carried out a few approaches to the drogue. This had showed up some quite serious deficiencies but at least the engineers had a good idea of what would be entailed. John Scott-Wilson, the Technical Director, had replied to the Ministry man that we could do it in a month, a quite outrageously short time. Normally such a modification would take a year at least but normal procurement procedures were being thrown out the window. Time was pressing; the Task Force was already at sea and needed the protection of maritime reconnaissance. The normal combat radius of the Nimrod is some 1,000 miles if one is to have a useful patrol time. From Ascension Island, where the task force was based, to the Falklands was 3,800 miles! Without the cover of the Nimrods the fleet would have no knowledge of enemy surface ships or, in particular, of enemy submarines. The assault would have to wait until we delivered the modified aircraft. The first delivery was made on May the first, not a month but a mere 18 days after that phone call.

XV229 was the first aircraft to be converted and, like all subsequent air-to-air refuelling capable Nimrods, was redesignated as the MR.2(P). First flown with the probe on 27 April, following further modifications the aircraft was back at Kinloss and the first operational sortie involving air-to-air refuelling was carried out by a No. 201 Squadron aircraft on 12 May. The sortie, which was planned to last for fifteen hours, included two refuellings and involved the support of six Handley Page Victor K.2 tankers, which also operated out of Wideawake. It was on this initial sortie that an Argentinean Navy Boeing 707 was spotted shadowing the British fleet, a situation that could not continue. The question asked of British Aerospace from the MoD was, 'How long would it take to fit and test Sidewinder missiles to the Nimrod?' A reply of just two weeks was given and an instruction to proceed was given straight away.

'Robby' Robinson was again heavily involved in the Sidewinder trials:

> The Nimrod had originally been designed to carry two SS.12 air-to-surface missiles under its wings. These had never gone into service so the requirement was deleted but the wiring

was still in situ, as were the wing reinforcement points. BAe Warton quickly designed the necessary pods and on 26 May Tony Banfield and I flew XV229 down to Boscombe Down where it was fitted with a pair of Sidewinders on each pod and we carried out a rapid series of tests to prove the handling qualities. On the morning of 27 May we flew to try out the acquisition mode of the missiles. This we did by flying up behind an unsuspecting civil aircraft and getting the characteristic growl in my headset that denoted that the missile had acquired its target; a noise I had never heard before, indeed I had never fired or carried a missile before in my life. With this aspect proved to our satisfaction we landed and the ground crew made the missiles live. We were now ready for the live firing. At the briefing it was made plain that this was to be a Company trial observed by the Boscombe Down pilot Tony Banfield. Tony was disappointed; he wanted the honour of being the first to fire a missile from the Nimrod. I compromised; I said that I would carry out the attack on the Jindivik drone target but that he could press the firing button. Not a big decision as the button on his side was the only one connected.

We took off and flew north until we reached Ailsa Craig, the small island between the Mull of Kintyre and Girvan on the West Coast of the mainland of Scotland. On the way I sneaked up behind a passing Victor tanker and tried out the acquisition growl. It worked. It was a beautiful day and we could see all the way to the Welsh coast from our 10,000 ft height. We began to circle the island, talking to RAE Aberporth who controlled the missile range that stretched to the south of us. They warned us that they were about to launch our target and read off the ranges to us as the little unmanned aircraft flew steadily south. I circled the aircraft tightly with all of the crew who could looking out to the north. After an anxious age Tony spotted it and I told Aberporth that we had it in sight. I swung our four-engined 'fighter' in behind the drone and Aberporth sent the signal to ignite the flare being towed behind the Jindivik. This flare was necessary, as the Sidewinder is a heat-seeking missile. We swiftly caught up with our target and as I heard the growl I told Tony to fire. To our utter surprise we were engulfed in a dense cloud of smoke and a deafening roar as the missile sped away. None of us had ever fired a missile before. As the Sidewinder neared its prey with its characteristic snake like motion the smoke cleared and we had a perfect view of the missile striking the flare. Complete success and so home for tea.

The sequel to our efforts was interesting. A few days after the flight Woodford was visited by a party of foreign guests. As they walked from the 748 that had brought them they happened to pass a Nimrod fully armed with four Sidewinders. A photograph was taken of the party, which appeared in the press the next day. In it one could clearly see the missiles. The Argentinean 707 was never seen again.

On top of the AIM-9 fit, the Nimrod's bomb bay could be modified to take cluster bombs and 1,000 lb retard bombs. The weapons system of the MR.2 was also upgraded to cater for a pair of AGM-84A-1 Harpoon anti-shipping missiles carried in the weapons bay.

Air-to-air refuelling procedures were hastily learnt by the Nimrod MR.2 crews and No. 206 Squadron, under the command of Wg Cdr D. Emmerson, flew some very long sorties. Nimrod MR.2 XV232, crewed by No. 201 Squadron, carried out a sortie that lasted nineteen hours and covered a distance of 8,300 miles on 15 May. Five days later, the same aircraft, now crewed by No. 206 Squadron, covered 8,453 miles in a little over eighteen hours!

111 sorties were flown by Nimrods during Operation Corporate in addition to No. 42 Squadron, which flew large numbers of SAR patrols operating from St Mawgan, Freetown (Sierra Leone) and Dakar (Senegal), providing cover to Harrier sorties to Ascension. No. 42 Squadron continued to provide SAR cover for RAF Hercules into Port Stanley after the conflict was over.

Above: No. 42 Squadron Nimrod MR.2 XV244, one of the first examples of the type to take part in Operation Corporate. Note the lack of refuelling probe. (Via J. D. Collectables)

Below: Nimrod XV258 which, along with XV244, flew the opening Nimrod sorties of the Falklands War. The aircraft is pictured at Yeovilton on 30 July 1982. (R. L. Ward)

Above: Nimrod MR.2 XV229, the first to be fitted with a refuelling probe. (Via R. L. Ward Collection)

Below: The crew of XV229 pose after the first flight of a Nimrod with a refuelling probe. Chief Test Pilot Wg Cdr J. A. 'Robby' Robinson is fifth from the left. (Via J. A. Robinson)

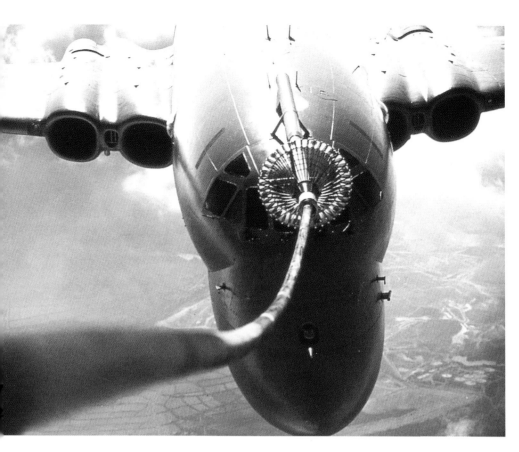

Above: An excellent view of a Nimrod MR.2 taking on fuel from a Handley Page Victor tanker. (Via J. A. Robinson)

Below: Nimrod MR.2 XV232 carried out the first 'wet' contacts with the new probe. The aircraft would go on to place a significant role during Operation Corporate. (Via J. A. Robinson)

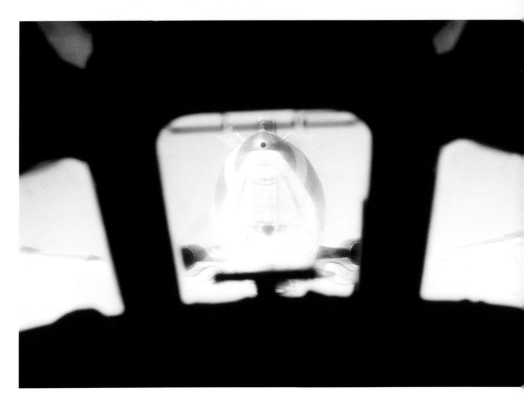

Above: And what it looks like from the cockpit! (Via J. A. Robinson)

Below: A Handley Page Victor K.2 of No. 57 Squadron refuelling a Nimrod MR.2, 30 April 1982.

Above: Incredibly rare image of a Nimrod firing a Sidewinder missile, making the aircraft, unofficially, the world's largest fighter! (Via J. A. Robinson)

Below: A number of Nimrod MR.2s were modified to carry a quartet of AIM-9L Sidewinder air-to-air missiles and they were more than happy for the public to see them, knowing that the information would reach the Argentine forces rather rapidly. (R. L. Ward)

Above: XV254, a Nimrod MR.2, during AIM-9 trials. (Via R. L. Ward Collection)

Below: Kinloss Wing Nimrod MR.2 XV234 shows off a Sidewinder at RAF Alconbury on 24 September 1983. (D. G. White via R. L. Ward Collection)

XV254, a Hawker Siddeley Nimrod MR.2 of the Kinloss Wing, off the Scottish coast. (British Aerospace, A14-1-945)

The Gulf War

With the invasion of Kuwait by Iraq, a detachment of three Nimrod MR.2s was despatched to Seeb, Oman, in August 1990 as part of Operation Desert Shield (the UK operation was called Operation Granby). The aircraft immediately began carrying out patrols over the Gulf of Oman and Persian Gulf but by the time hostilities began proper, as part of Operation Desert Storm in January 1991, the Nimrod detachment had increased to five aircraft. The RAF contingent mainly flew night-time operations while the US Navy's P-3 Orion covered the daylight patrols. One of many tasks carried out by the Nimrod MR.2 was to guide British Army (Army Air Corps) and Royal Navy Westland Lynx attack helicopters (operating as part of SUCAP (Surface Unit CAP)) and US Navy A-6 Intruder aircraft towards Iraqi patrol vessels, of which British forces can be credited with sinking or damaging sixteen vessels. Four of these targets were identified in one day, on 21 January. In early February Nimrods were cleared to operate over the northern Gulf. Each night a Nimrod would fly a figure-of-eight pattern at medium altitude, 30 miles away from the Kuwaiti coast. Small resupply vessels could be picked up in this area, especially close to Faylaka Island. Following the start of the ground war on 23 February, Nimrod sorties reduced to one per day, but would continue into March, long after the Iraqi Army surrendered.

No. 51 Squadron's Nimrod R.1s, operating from Akrotiri, flew continuous operations from August 1990 through to March 1991. The R.1s by this time, for their own defence, were fitted with chaff and flare pods and BOZ pods. During the Gulf War, Nimrod MR.2s were credited with flying sixty-seven missions while the Nimrod R.1 chalked up eighty.

Nimrods were also involved in supporting NATO forces against Serbia in 1993 and in 2003. No. 51 Squadron would return to the Middle East in 1998 when a single aircraft was deployed to Kuwait International Airport prior to the launch of the US-named Operation Desert Fox. No. 51 Squadron also played its part during the war in Kosovo in 1999 when a single aircraft operated out of Practica di Mare, Lazio, Italy.

Afghanistan

Following the terrorist attack on the World Trade Centre on 11 September 2001, the United States began operations in Afghanistan in an attempt to destroy Al-Qaeda. US operations began on 9 October, the RAF providing air-to-air refuelling support for the US Navy and AEW support via Nos 8 and 23 Squadrons. The Nimrod MR.2 was also deployed to fly maritime patrols over the Indian Ocean, again in support of the US Navy. As with most modern conflicts, No. 51 Squadron were also involved, their Nimrod R.1s being used for electronic surveillance.

No. 51 Squadron returned to Afghanistan in 2009 as part of Operation Panchai Palang, a coalition effort to remove the Taliban once and for all. Operating out of Seeb, the Nimrod R.1 was now referred to as an ISTAR (Intelligence, Surveillance, Target Acquisition and Reconnaissance) asset and was now operating alongside No. 5 Squadron's new aircraft, the Sentinel R.1.

The final operation that the Nimrod R.1 involved in was Libya in 2011, a situation the aircraft's time in service had been extended for. Before being withdrawn, the hard-working aircraft had flown nearly 350 hours in support of operations.

Operation Telic

A very well-organised response by the RAF to the next round of operations in Iraq began in late 2002. The Nimrod was once again involved as part of a large deployment to the Prince Sultan Air Base in Saudi Arabia. Four Nimrod MR.2s belonging to Nos 120, 201 and 206 Squadrons were joined by the obligatory single Nimrod R.1 provided by No. 51 Squadron.

Conclusion

The Nimrod MR.2 was the perfect aircraft for locating hostile forces and controlling attacks on those forces by coalition forces. From the outset, though, the Nimrod was designed for maritime patrol but the Iraq and Afghanistan campaigns saw the goalposts move for the aircraft and more demand was placed upon it to fly long reconnaissance missions overland. Inevitably, the already old airframes suffered as a result and the cost and disruption of retraining the crews in the maritime role when they returned to the United Kingdom did not help the situation.

Prior to 2006, four aircraft had been lost in accidents: Nimrod MR.2 XV256 by bird strike; Nimrod MR.2 XV257 was written off following a flare igniting in the weapons bay; the ditching of Nimrod R.1 XW666; and the loss of Nimrod MR.2 XV230 during the Canadian International Air Show over Lake Ontario. None of these incidents had the effect of what occurred to Nimrod MR.2 XV230 on 2 September 2006. The first of the breed to be converted from a MR.1 to an MR.2, XV230 had given faultless service up to this point, when it inexplicably exploded and crashed near Kandahar, killing all fourteen on board. Rumour as to what caused the explosion ran away with itself and then politics got involved, which is never good news. Early indications that the problem occurred with the fuel pumps would not, at first, be confirmed by the MoD and in the meantime Nimrod operations continued. Still unable to confirm if the fuel pumps were the problem, the MoD decided to ground all Nimrod MR.2s pending further investigations on 23 February 2007. A number of modifications were implemented to the fuel pumps and fuel transfer systems. However, the first of several nails in the coffin for the aircraft came on 5 November 2007

Kinloss Wing
Nimrod MR.2
XV255 on patrol.
(Via R. L. Ward
Collection)

Above: A Nimrod MR.2 from the Kinloss Wing shadows a Royal Navy submarine during an exercise. (Crown Copyright via Chris Hearn)

Below: A regular sight at RAF Akrotiri, Cyprus; this example of the 'Mighty Hunter' is Kinloss Wing Nimrod MR.2 XV245, pictured on 2 November 1988. (R. L. Ward)

Right: Nimrod MR.2 XV255 in company with No. 13 Squadron (RAF Marham) and No. 617 Squadron (RAF Lossiemouth) Tornado GR.1s off the Scottish coast in 1994. (Crown Copyright via Chris Hearn)

Below: A nice study of Nimrod MR.2 XV260. (Crown Copyright via Chris Hearn)

Nimrod MR.2 XV252 takes on fuel from No. 101 Squadron VC10 K.2 ZA143 'D'. (Crown Copyright via Chris Hearn)

Nimrod MR.2 XV255 keeps a close watch on a fishing trawler in the North Sea. (Via Harry Holmes)

No. 120 Squadron Nimrod MR.2 XV240 during a gathering at RAF Marham on 30 March 1993. (Via Chris Hearn)

Nimrod MR.2 XV254 tucks up close enough so you can see its twenty-fifth anniversary markings in 1994. (Crown Copyright via Chris Hearn)

Kinloss Wing Nimrod MR.2 XV238 over Forres; the aircraft was retired and scrapped nearby in Elgin in 1991. (Crown Copyright via Chris Hearn)

Kinloss Wing Nimrod MR.2 XV230 on finals into RAF Fairford for RIAT on 19 July 1997. (R. L. Ward)

Kinloss Wing
Nimrod MR.2
XV235 tucks up
early after take-off
at Yeovilton on
16 July 1994.
(R. L. Ward)

Kinloss Wing
Nimrod MR.2
XV231 at rest
at RAF Kinloss
on 20 July 1995.
(Crown Copyright
(No.1414-01) via
Chris Hearn)

RAF Marham
flypast; this
Nimrod MR.2 is in
formation with two
No. 29 Squadron
Canberra T.4s
on 29 May 2002.
(Crown Copyright
via Chris Hearn)

An aerial view of RAF Kinloss in the 1990s with at least fourteen Nimrod MR.2s visible, although not all are airworthy. The station was the home of the Nimrod from 1969 until 2011. (Crown Copyright via Chris Hearn)

when Nimrod MR.2 XV235 was carrying out air-to-air refuelling over Afghanistan. A leak was detected by the crew but this time, after transmitting a Mayday call, the aircraft landed safely. Only four weeks before the Board of Enquiry report was published into the loss of XV230, which was most likely lost in a similar incident, the RAF decided to suspend all Nimrod air-to-air refuelling.

By now the politicians were running wild with the story and several high-profile individuals called for the aircraft to be grounded and then withdrawn from service. They got their wish; it was all over by the summer of 2011 and a colossal gap in the RAF's capability was exposed, exacerbated by the scrapping of the Nimrod MRA.4 before it even entered service. Once again, though, the RAF would look across the Pond for the solution, where it was presented with the Boeing P-8 Poseidon, a multi-mission maritime aircraft based upon the 737-800 airliner. Nine aircraft were ordered in 2016 at a cost of £3 billion, the first of which, designated the Poseidon MRA.4, first flew on 13 July 2019 and was received by the RAF at Boeing's Seattle plant on 29 October. The aircraft will be operated from RAF Lossiemouth by No. 120 Squadron by the spring of 2020.

Preserved Aircraft

MR.1 (Mod)

XV148
Cockpit preserved at Malmesbury

MR.2

XV226
Delivered to Bruntingthorpe on 27 April 2010.

No. 42 Squadron Nimrod MR.2 XV226 during a spirited display at the RAF Mildenhall Air Fete on 23 May 1992. (R. L. Ward)

XV229

WFU on 31 March 2020 and now resides at the Fire Training School at Manston.

Above: No. 206 Squadron Nimrod MR.2 XV229 provides an interesting foreground as Liberator *Diamond Lil* arrives in the background at RAF Kinloss in 1992. (Crown Copyright via Chris Hearn)

Below: In service with No. 201 Squadron, Nimrod MR.2 XV229 is seen on the static line at RAF Fairford on 20 July 1991. (R. L. Ward)

XV231
Delivered to Manchester Airport for display on 21 April 2010.

Above: A regular visitor to RAF Fairford during the air show season, this No. 206 Squadron Nimrod MR.2, XV231, is seen on 19 July 1996. (R. L. Ward)

Below: Families Day at RAF Honington and Nimrod MR.2 XV231 puts on a display on 27 June 1992. (R. L. Ward)

XV232
Delivered to Coventry Airport on 11 May 2010 for preservation.

Above: Nimrod MR.2 XV232, pictured in tropical climes; the aircraft is preserved at Coventry today in 'working order'. (Crown Copyright via Chris Hearn)

Below: Mildenhall Air Fete again, and this time it is the turn of Nimrod MR.2 XV232 to put on a show on 26 May 1990. (R. L. Ward)

XV235

Forward fuselage preserved outside the Avro Heritage Centre, Woodford. Aircraft WFU on 31 March 2000.

XV240

Forward fuselage preserved at ex-RAF Kinloss by Morayvia; had served as a gate guard since 9 September 2009.

XV244

Complete aircraft preserved at ex-RAF Kinloss by Morayvia having been WFU on 31 March 2010.

Above: A Kinloss Wing Nimrod MR.2 at RAF Brize Norton on 5 June 1993. (R. L. Ward)

Left: Nimrod MR.2 XV244 put on a good show at RAF Marham on 30 March 1993. To the rear are an ATM-84A-1C Harpoon anti-ship missile and a pair of CLEs (Container Land Equipment). The contents of the latter vary depending on the environment, hence 'Desert' on the side of the CLE in the centre of the image. (R. L. Ward)

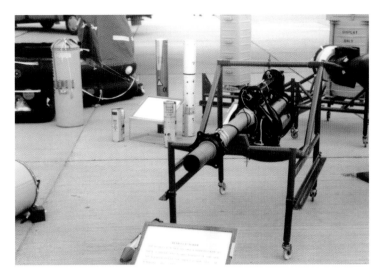

More kit on display near XV244, including a Retro Launcher which allowed a Nimrod crew to drop a smoke and flame marker in the sea. The marker burns for approximately ten minutes and they were used for anti-submarine and ASR operations. (R. L. Ward)

XV250
WFU 13 March 2010 and delivered to the Yorkshire Air Museum, Elvington, on 13 April 2010 for preservation.

XV254
Nose section to Highland Aviation Museum, Inverness, in April 2010.

XV255
Delivered to the Norwich Air Museum on 24 May 2010.

Nimrod MR.2 XV255 undergoing maintenance at RAF Kinloss. (BAE Systems via R. L. Ward Collection)

Ex-No. 51 Squadron Nimrod R.1 XV249 on display at RAF Cosford; the aircraft made its final flight on 28 June 2011. (Andy King)

Striking night-time view of Nimrod R.1 XV249. (Andy King)

R.1

XV249
Final flight on 29 July 2011 from Waddington to Kemble, from where it was dismantled and delivered by road to the RAF Museum at Cosford on 11 March 2012.

XW664
WFU in June 2011 and delivered to East Midlands Aeropark, East Midlands Airport, on 12 July 2011.

XW666
Nose section, Long Marston (Oct. 1999), now at Aeroventure, Doncaster.

XW666, a Nimrod R.1 of No. 51 Squadron, around 1988. (Via R. L. Ward Collection)

AEW.3

XV259
Nose section at the Solway Aviation Museum. Aircraft was broken up at Stock, Essex, in October 1998.

MRA.4

ZJ515
Scrapped at Woodford on 24 February 2011 although nose section is believed to have been moved to Cranfield in March 2011.

XV259, a Nimrod AEW.3, at Abingdon around 1989. (R. L. Ward)

Technical Specifications

Nimrod (Trials Aircraft)

Serials: XV147 (c/n 6476) and XV148 (c/n 6477)
MinTech modified from Comet 4Cs and delivered in May and Jul. 1967 to Contract KD/G/64.

MR.1

Serials: XV226–XV263 (thirty-eight aircraft delivered between July 1968 and August 1972 by HAS, Woodford, to Contract KD/G/64) and XZ280–XZ287 (eight aircraft delivered by HAS, Woodford, to Contract KA/2B/38 – XZ285–XZ287 were delivered as MR.2s)
Engine: Four 12,150 lb (or 11,500 lb?) Rolls-Royce RB 168 Spey 250 turbofans
Dimensions: Span, 114 ft 10 in.; Length, 129 ft 9 in.; Height, 32 ft 9 in.; Wing Area, 2,121 sq/ft
Weights: Empty, 86,000 lb; Loaded, 196,410 lb
Performance: Max speed, 574 mph; Cruising speed, 490 mph; Range, up to 5,755 miles; Endurance, twelve hours; Service ceiling, 42,000 ft
Crew: Twelve
Armament: A variety of sonobouys, bombs, mines, nuclear depth chargers, torpedoes and potentially AS.12 and Martel missiles

MR.2 and MR.2P

Serials: All conversions from MR.1 – XV226–XV251 (MR.2P), XV252–XV260 (MR.2P), XZ284, XZ285*, XZ286*, XZ287* (thirty-five)
Engine: Four 12,160 lb Rolls-Royce RB 168-20 Spey 250 turbofans
Dimensions: Span, 114 ft 10 in.; Length, 129 ft 1 in.; Height, 29 ft 8.5 in.; Wing Area, 2,121 sq/ft
Weights: Empty, 86,000 lb; Loaded, 192,000 lb
Performance: Max speed, 575 mph; Cruising speed, 490 mph; Range, up to 5,755 miles; Endurance, twelve hours; Service ceiling, 42,000 ft
Crew: Up to twenty-four
Armament: Nine Mk 44 or Mk 46 homing torpedoes (or Marconi Stingray torpedoes) in bomb bay, or alternatively nuclear depth charges or conventional 1,000 lb iron bombs; provision to carry two Harpoon air-to-surface missiles and up to four AIM-9 Sidewinders for self-defence

*New-build MR.2s

R.1

Serials: XV249 (Converted MR.2 in 1995/96), XW664–XW666 (three aircraft delivered between July 1971 and August 1972 by HSA, Woodford, to Contract KD/G/93)
Engine: Four 12,160 lb Rolls-Royce Spey turbofans
Dimensions: Span, 114 ft 10 in.; Length, 118 ft; Height, 29 ft 9 in.; Wing Area, 2,121 sq/ft
Weights: Empty, *c.* 86,000 lb; Loaded, *c.* 192,000 lb
Performance: Max speed, 575 mph; Cruising speed, 490 mph; Range, up to 5,755 miles; Service ceiling, 44,000 ft
Crew: Up to twenty-nine

AEW.3

Serials: XV259, XV261, XV262, XV263, XZ280–XZ283 (All ex-MR.1s) and XZ285–XZ287 (Ex-MR.2s)
Engine: Four 12,140 lb Rolls-Royce RB 168-20 turbofans
Dimensions: Span, 115 ft 1 in.; Length, 137 ft 8.5 in.; Height, 35 ft; Wing Area, 2,121 sq/ft
Weights: Empty, 86,000 lb; Max Take-off, 187,800 lb
Performance: Service ceiling, 36,000 ft
Crew: Twelve

MRA.4

Serials: ZJ517–ZJ534
Engines: Four 15,500 lb Rolls-Royce/BMW Deutschland BR710 turbofans
Dimensions: Span, 127 ft; Length, 126 ft 9 in.; Height, 31 ft; Wing Area, 2,538 sq/ft
Weights: Empty, 114,000 lb; Max Take-off, 232,315 lb
Performance: Max speed, 571 mph; Range, 6,910 miles; Service ceiling, 36,000 ft
Crew: Ten
Armament: Four underwing pylons and an internal bomb bay capable of holding 22,000 lb; combinations of the following could be carried – Two AIM-9 Sidewinder; AGM-65 Maverick; AGM-84 Harpoon; Storm Shadow; depth charges; Mk 46 torpedoes; Sting Ray torpedoes, naval mines; and sonobuoys

RAF Nimrod Units & Operators

No. 42 Sqn	*Fortiter in re,* 'Bravely into action'
A/c	MR.1: April 1971 to June 1984
	MR.2 and 2P: June 1983 to April 2011
Dates	Nimrod replaced Shackleton MR.3 at St Mawgan; DB from front-line in October 1992; RF as No. 42(Reserve) Sqn at Kinloss, taking over No. 236 OCU duties until DB 26 May 2011.
Stations	St Mawgan 8 October 1958; Kinloss April 1982; St Mawgan 1 November 1983; Kinloss 31 July 1992
Cos	Wg Cdr B. W. Lofthouse (Dec. 1969); Wg Cdr D. W. Hann (Aug. 1972); Wg Cdr T. H. Watson (Sep 1974); Wg Cdr A. G. Hicks (Jul. 1976); Wg Cdr D. R. Green (Jan. 1978); Wg Cdr D. L. Bough (Jan 1982); Wg Cdr R. W. Joseph (1990); Wg Cdr C. J. Lawrence (1994); Wg Cdr T. Bennington (2004)

Nimrod MR.1 XV256 of No. 42 Squadron puts on a show at RAF St Mawgan on 22 March 1973. The cavernous near 50-foot-long weapons bay is clear for all to see. (R. L. Ward)

No. 51 Squadron Nimrod R.1 XW664 taxying for take-off at RAF Waddington. (R. L. Ward)

No. 51 Sqn	Swift and Sure
A/c	MR.1: *c.* 1976 to *c.* 1978
	R.1: July 1971 to 2011
Dates	Nimrod joined No. 51 Sqn as an addition to the resident Canberra B.6 and Comet C.2(R) until the former departed in Oct 1976 and the latter in Jan 1975; replaced by the Boeing RC-135W Rivet Joint in 2014
Stations	Wyton (31 March 1963); Waddington (1995)
COs	Wg Cdr G. J. B. Claridge (Mar. 1971); Wg Cdr W. H. Bonner (Dec. 1972); Wg Cdr R. H. Wood (Dec 1974); Wg Cdr M. Arnold (Mar. 1977); Wg Cdr D. H. Barnes (Sep. 1979); Wg Cdr B. N. J. Speed (Oct. 1981); Wg Cdr E. W. Tyack (Sep. 1983); Wg Cdr P. R. Jeffers (Dec. 1985); Wg Cdr M. L. Feenan (Dec. 1988); Wg Cdr P. M. Blee (Mar. 1991); Wg Cdr P. J. J. Haines (Sep. 1993); Wg Cdr B. A. Smith (May 1996); Wg Cdr D. Paton; Wg Cdr K. Havelock (2001); Wg Cdr N. Sharpe (2004); Wg Cdr G. Crosby; Wg Cdr T. Talbot

120 Sqn	Endurance
A/c	MR.1: October 1970 to February 1982
	MR.2: April 1981 to March 2010
Dates	Nimrod replaced Shackleton MR.3 at Kinloss from Oct 1970; Nimrod MR.2 was withdrawn on 31 March 2010, unit DB on 26 May 2011
Stations	Kinloss (1 April 1959)
COs	Wg Cdr A. R. Amos (Apr. 1969); Wg Cdr C. J. Philips (Dec. 1971); Wg Cdr R. Kidney (Jan 1974); Wg Cdr T. C. Flanagan (Dec 1975); Wg Cdr C. J. Sturt (Oct 1977); Wg Cdr M. G. Peakes (Nov. 1979); Wg Cdr W. Metcalfe

No. 120 Squadron's anniversary aircraft, Nimrod MR.2 XV240. (R. L. Ward)

201 Sqn	*Hic et ubique,* 'Here and everywhere'
A/c	MR.1: July 1970 to February 1983
	MR.2: January 1982 to March 2010
Dates	Nimrod replaced Shackleton MR.3 at Kinloss from July 1970; DB 26 May
2011	
Stations	Kinloss (1 July 1965)
COs	Wg Cdr J. B. Duxbury (Mar. 1971); Wg Cdr J. M. Alcock (Oct. 1971); Wg Cdr J. Morris (Aug. 1975); Wg Cdr P. M. Stean (Aug. 1977); Wg Cdr A. W. J. Stewart (1993); Wg Cdr A. D. Fryer (Jun. 2001); Wg Cdr J. C. McG Johnston (Dec. 2003)

No. 201 Squadron Nimrod MR.1 XV250 on finals to land at RAF Finningley in July 1977. (R. L. Ward)

No. 203 Squadron Nimrod MR.1 XV263 on finals to land at RAF Luqa in 1978. (R. L. Ward)

203 Sqn	*Occidens oriensque,* 'West and east'
A/c	MR.1: October 1971 to 31 December 1977
Dates	Nimrod replaced the Shackleton MR.3 at Luqa, Malta, in October 1971; DB 31 December 1977
Stations	Luqa (1 February 1969); Sigonella (12 January 1972); Luqa (23 April 1972)
COs	Wg Cdr R. G. Bowyer (Nov. 1968); Wg Cdr A. J. Freeborn (Nov. 1971); Wg Cdr G. A. King (May 1974); Wg Cdr G. K. Peasley (Jan. 1975); Wg Cdr J. H. Carter (Sep. 1976)

206 Sqn	*Nihil nos effugit,* 'Nothing escapes us'
A/c	MR.1: August 1970 to February 1981
	MR.2: February 1980 to April 2005
Dates	Nimrod replaced Shackleton MR.3 at Kinloss from August 1970; DB April 2005
Stations	Kinloss (1 July 1965)
COs	Wg Cdr J. Wild (May 1970); Wg Cdr M. J. W. Pierson; Wg Cdr J. Wild; Wg Cdr R. C. McKinlay (Apr. 1979); Wg Cdr D. Emmerson (May 1981); Wg Cdr R. W. Joseph; Wg Cdr S. D. Butler (Jul. 1994); Wg Cdr T. Cross (1999); Wg Cdr R. Noel (*c.* 2003)

An early flight of XV228 as a newly converted Nimrod MR.2 over the Moray Firth, not far from RAF Kinloss, in September 1982. (British Aerospace Manchester A13-1-196 via J. D. Collectables)

Nimrod MR.1 XV230, in service with No. 236 OCU out of RAF St Mawgan, back in 1969. (Via J. D. Collectables)

236 OCU	*Imprimis Praecepta*, 'Our teaching is everlasting'
A/c	MR.1: July 1970 to *c.* 1980
	MR.2: *c.* 1980 to October 1992
Dates	MOTU at St Mawgan reverted 1 July 1970 to being No. 236 OCU in 18 Group to train Nimrod crews, also known as No. 38(R) Sqn; 1 May 1982 temp at Kinloss during runway resurfacing; 18 Jan. 1984 returned to St Mawgan; DB 1 Oct. 1992 and tasking to No. 42 (Reserve) Sqn at Kinloss
Stations	St Mawgan (Jul. 1970); Kinloss (May 1982); St Mawgan (Jan. 1984)

A&AEE
A/c: Nimrod – XV148*; MR.1 – XV226, XV227, XV228, XV229, XV239, XV250, XV251, XW665, XZ283; MR.2 – XV227, XV229, XV239, XV241, XV242, XV254, XZ284; MR.2P – XZ284; R.1 – XW664, XW665; AEW.3 – XZ285 and XZ286

*Operated by unit on two separate occasions

BAe
A/c: Nimrod – XV147, XV148; MR.2 – XV244, XV249; MR.2P – XV251; AEW.3 – XV259, XV261, XV262, XZ280, XZ281 and XZ282

HSA
A/c: Nimrod – XV147 and XV148

Kinloss Wing
A/c: MR.1 – XV226, XV227, XV228, XV229, XV230, XV231, XV232, XV233, XV235, XV236*, XV238, XV239*, XV240***, XV241*, XV242*, XV243, XV244*, XV245*, XV246*,

XV247*, XV248*, XV249*, XV250*, XV251, XV252*, XV253, XV254, XV255, XV256, XV257, XV258, XV259, XV261***, XV262, XZ280, XZ281, XZ282*; MR.2 – XV226, XV227, XV228, XV229, XV230, XV231, XV232, XV233, XV234, XV235, XV236, XV237**, XV238**, XV239**, XV240**, XV241**, XV242**, XV243**, XV244, XV245, XV246, XV247, XV248, XV249, XV250**, XV252, XV253**, XV254**, XV255, XV256, XV257**, XV258, XZ284****; MR.2P – XV251

*Served with unit on two separate occasions as an MR.1
**Served with unit on two separate occasions as an MR.2
***Served with unit on three separate occasions as an MR.1
***Served with unit on three separate occasions as an MR.2

MinTech
A/c: MR.1 – XV226, XV228 and XV229

Mod(PE)
A/c: MR.2P – XV251; R.1 – XW665

Nimrod AEW JTU
Formed 18 December 1984 from the Training Squadron and the A&AEE Nimrod Trials Team at Waddington; DB April 1987
A/c: AEW.3 – XZ263, XZ285, XZ286 and XZ287

Nimrod Major Servicing Unit
Formed 1 February 1972 in 18 Group at Kinloss; Contractorised 6 June 1995

RAE
A/c: Nimrod – XV147

RRE
A/c: Nimrod – XV148

RSRE
A/c: Nimrod – XV148

St Mawgan Wing
A/c: MR.1 – XV226, XV234, XV235, XV237, XV253, XV254, XV255, XV256, XV259, XZ282; MR.2 – XV226, XV227, XV228, XV229, XV231, XV232, XV233, XV234, XV235, XV236, XV237, XV240, XV241, XV242, XV243, XV245, XV246, XV248, XV249, XV252, XV253, XV257, XV258, XZ284*, XZ285; MR.2P – XV251

*Served with unit on two separate occasions as an MR.2

Glossary

A&AEE	Aircraft and Armament Experimental Establishment
AEW	Airborne Early Warning
AEWTU	Airborne Early Warning Training Unit
AOC-in-C	Air Officer Commanding-in-Chief
ASRAAM	Advanced Short Range Air-to-Air Missiles
ASR	Air Staff Requirement/Air Sea Rescue
ASV	Air Surface Vessel
AUTEC	Atlantic Undersea Test and Evaluation Centre
AW	Armstrong Whitworth
BAC	British Aircraft Corporation
BAe	British Aerospace
BOAC	British Overseas Airways Corporation
BOZ	Bofors – Type Z
CO	Commanding Officer
DB	Disbanded
ECM	Electronic Counter Measures
EEC	European Economic Community
ELINT	Electronic Intelligence
EMI	Electrical & Musical Industries
ESM	Electronic Support Measures
GI	Ground Instruction
HAS	Hawker Siddeley Aviation
HF	High Frequency
HS	Hawker Siddeley
ICG	Icelandic Coastguard
IFR	In-flight Refuelling
JTU	Joint Trials Unit
MAD	Magnetic Anomaly Detector
MIL-STD	Military Standard
MinTech	Ministry of Technology
MoD	Ministry of Defence
MOTU	Maritime Operational Training Unit
MR	Maritime Reconnaissance
MRA	Maritime Reconnaissance and Anti-Submarine
NATO	North Atlantic Treaty Organisation
OCU	Operational Conversion Unit
OR	Operational Requirement

PM	Prime Minister
R	Reconnaissance
RAE	Royal Aircraft Establishment
RDD	Routine Dynamic Display)
RRE	Radar Research Establishment
RSRE	Royal Signals and Radar Establishment
SIGINT	Signals Intelligence
SLAM-ER	Standoff Land Attack Missile – Expanded Response
TEU	Trials Evaluation Unit
VC	Vickers Commercial
WFU	Withdrawn from Use

Bibliography

Flintham, Vic, *High Stakes: Britain's Air Arms in Action, 1945–90* (Pen & Sword Aviation)

Halley, James J. (ed.), *RAF Aircraft XA100–XZ999* (Air Britain)

Jefford, C. G., *RAF Squadrons* (Airlife)

Napier, Michael, *The Royal Air Force – A Centenary of Operations* (Osprey)

Noble, Bernard (ed.), *Properly to Test*, Book Two (Old Forge)

Robinson, J. A., *Avro One, Autobiography of a Chief Test Pilot* (Old Forge)

Sturtivant, Ray, *RAF Flying Training and Support Units since 1912* (Air Britain)

Thetford, Owen, *Aircraft of the Royal Air Force since 1918* (Putnam)

Wilson, Michael, 'Hawker Siddeley Nimrod MR.1' (*Flight*, 13 June 1968)

Spyflight – www.spyflight.co.uk